# FUNDAMENTALS OF DATABASE DESIGN

# FUNDAMENTALS OF DATABASE DESIGN

**BY**

**GRACE RYAN**
**DANIAN DAY**

KNOWLEDGE BAKERS

ISBN: 9789390013050 (HB)



*Published by* : **Knowledge Bakers**
Pune, India
*Email: knowledgebakers2019@gmail.com*

*Digitally Printed at* : **Replika Press Pvt. Ltd.**

# PREFACE

It is a representation of some aspect of the real world or a collection of data elements (facts) representing real-world information. A database is logical, coherent and internally consistent. A database is designed, built and populated with data for a specific purpose. Each data item is stored in a field. A database is a collection of data that is organized in a way that allows for efficient storage, retrieval, and manipulation. Database design is the process of creating a structure for a database that is optimized for the specific needs of the organization or individual using it. We will discuss the fundamentals of database design, including the purpose of a database, the importance of data normalization, and the use of database management systems (DBMS). Data, such as customer information, product details, financial records, and more. A well-designed database allows for efficient storage, retrieval, and manipulation of data. This, in turn, leads to increased productivity, reduced errors, and better decision-making.

One of the most important concepts in database design is data normalization. Data normalization is the process of organizing data in a database so that it is structured in a way that reduces redundancy and improves data integrity. This is achieved by breaking down large tables into smaller, more specific tables that are linked together by key fields. This process helps to eliminate data inconsistencies and reduces the likelihood of errors. A database management system (DBMS) is a software application that is used to manage data in a database. DBMS provides an interface between the user and the database, allowing for easy access to the data stored within. DBMS can also perform functions such as data backup and recovery, data encryption, and data security.

The book covers fundamental concepts such as data, information, metadata, and database. It explains the differences between these terms and how they are interconnected. The book explores the characteristics of a database system and its benefits, such as data independence, data security, and efficient data access. The book covers the entity-relationship data model, which is a widely used modelling technique for designing relational databases. It explains the concepts of entities, attributes, and relationships. The book describes the importance of maintaining data integrity in a database system and explains how to enforce integrity rules and constraints. The book covers ER modelling, explains how to create an ER diagram and explores the concept of functional dependencies and how they are used in database design. The book covers SQL's data manipulation language, which includes statements used for inserting, updating, and deleting data in a database. This book is intended for computer science majors and the study matter lays special emphasis on designs issues, relational calculus, mathematical models and relational algebra.

We are grateful to all those persons as well as various books, manuals, periodicals, magazines, journals etc. that helped in the preparation of this book. In spite of the best efforts, it is possible that some errors may have occurred into the compilation and editing of the book. Further queries, constructive suggestions and criticisms for the improvement of the book are always welcomed and shall be thankfully acknowledged.

**Grace Ryan**
**Danian Day**

# CONTENTS

# Chapter 1 Before the Advent of Database Systems

The way in which computers manage data has come a long way over the last few decades. Today's users take for granted the many benefits found in a database system. However, it wasn't that long ago that computers relied on a much less elegant and costly approach to data management called the file-based system.

## File-based System

One way to keep information on a computer is to store it in permanent files. A company system has a number of application programs; each of them is designed to manipulate data files. These application programs have been written at the request of the users in the organization. New applications are added to the system as the need arises. The system just described is called the *file-based system.*

Consider a traditional banking system that uses the file-based system to manage the organization's data shown in Figure 1.1. As we can see, there are different departments in the bank. Each has its own applications that manage and manipulate different data files. For banking systems, the programs may be used to debit or credit an account, find the balance of an account, add a new mortgage loan and generate monthly statements.

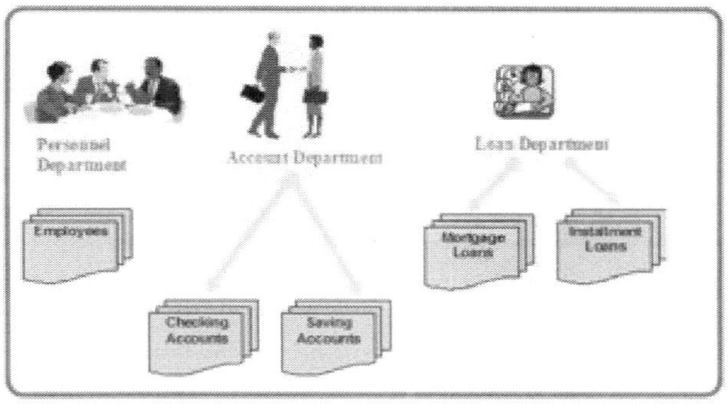


*Figure 1.1. Example of a file-based system used by banks to manage data.*

### Disadvantages of the file-based approach

Using the file-based system to keep organizational information has a number of disadvantages. Listed below are five examples.

#### *Data redundancy*

Often, within an organization, files and applications are created by different programmers from various departments over long periods of time. This can lead to *data redundancy*, a situation that occurs in a database when a field needs to be updated in more than one table. This practice can lead to several problems such as:

- Inconsistency in data format
- The same information being kept in several different places (files)
- *Data inconsistency*, a situation where various copies of the same data are conflicting, wastes storage space and duplicates effort

### *Data isolation*

*Data isolation* is a property that determines when and how changes made by one operation become visible to other concurrent users and systems. This issue occurs in a concurrency situation. This is a problem because:

- It is difficult for new applications to retrieve the appropriate data, which might be stored in various files.

### *Integrity problems*

Problems with *data integrity* is another disadvantage of using a file-based system. It refers to the maintenance and assurance that the data in a database are correct and consistent. Factors to consider when addressing this issue are:

- Data values must satisfy certain consistency constraints that are specified in the application programs.
- It is difficult to make changes to the application programs in order to enforce new constraints.

### *Security problems*

Security can be a problem with a file-based approach because:

- There are constraints regarding accessing privileges.
- Application requirements are added to the system in an ad-hoc manner so it is difficult to enforce constraints.

### *Concurrency access*

*Concurrency* is the ability of the database to allow multiple users access to the same record without adversely affecting transaction processing. A file-based system must manage, or prevent, concurrency by the application programs. Typically, in a file-based system, when an application opens a file, that file is locked. This means that no one else has access to the file at the same time.

In database systems, concurrency is managed thus allowing multiple users access to the same record. This is an important difference between database and file-based systems.

## Database Approach

The difficulties that arise from using the file-based system have prompted the development of a new approach in managing large amounts of organizational information called the *database approach*.

Databases and database technology play an important role in most areas where computers are used, including business, education and medicine. To understand the fundamentals of database systems, we will start by introducing some basic concepts in this area.

## Role of databases in business

Everybody uses a database in some way, even if it is just to store information about their friends and family. That data might be written down or stored in a computer by using a word-processing program or it could be saved in a spreadsheet. However, the best way to store data is by using *database management software*. This is a powerful software tool that allows you to store, manipulate and retrieve data in a variety of different ways.

Most companies keep track of customer information by storing it in a database. This data may include customers, employees, products, orders or anything else that assists the business with its operations.

## The meaning of data

Data are factual information such as measurements or statistics about objects and concepts. We use data for discussions or as part of a calculation. Data can be a person, a place, an event, an action or any one of a number of things. A single fact is an element of data, or a *data element*.

If data are information and information is what we are in the business of working with, you can start to see where you might be storing it. Data can be stored in:

- Filing cabinets
- Spreadsheets
- Folders
- Ledgers
- Lists
- Piles of papers on your desk

All of these items store information, and so too does a database. Because of the mechanical nature of databases, they have terrific power to manage and process the information they hold. This can make the information they house much more useful for your work.

With this understanding of data, we can start to see how a tool with the capacity to store a collection of data and organize it, conduct a rapid search, retrieve and process, might make a difference to how we can use data. This book and the chapters that follow are all about managing information.

*Key Terms*

**concurrency**: the ability of the database to allow multiple users access to the same record without adversely affecting transaction processing

**data element**: a single fact or piece of information

**data inconsistency**: a situation where various copies of the same data are conflicting

**data isolation**: a property that determines when and how changes made by one operation become visible to other concurrent users and systems

**data integrity**: refers to the maintenance and assurance that the data in a database are correct and consistent

**data redundancy**: a situation that occurs in a database when a field needs to be updated in more than one table

**database approach**: allows the management of large amounts of organizational information

**database management software**: a powerful software tool that allows you to store, manipulate and retrieve data in a variety of ways

**file-based system**: an application program designed to manipulate data files

*Exercises*

1. Discuss each of the following terms:
    1. data
    2. field
    3. record
    4. file
2. What is data redundancy?
3. Discuss the disadvantages of file-based systems.
4. Explain the difference between data and information.
5. Use Figure 1.2 (below) to answer the following questions.
    1. In the table, how many records does the file contain?
    2. How many fields are there per record?
    3. What problem would you encounter if you wanted to produce a listing by city?
    4. How would you solve this problem by altering the file structure?

| PROJECT_CODE | PROJECT_MANAGER | MANAGER_PHONE | MANAGER_ADDRESS | PROJECT_BID_PRICE |
|---|---|---|---|---|
| 21-5Z | Holly B. Parker | 904-338-3416 | 3334 Lee Rd., Gainesville, FL 37123 | $16,833,460.00 |
| 25-2D | Jane D. Grant | 615-898-9909 | 218 Clark Blvd., Nashville, TN 36362 | $12,500,000.00 |
| 25-5A | George F. Dorts | 615-227-1245 | 124 River Dr., Franklin, TN 29185 | $32,512,420.00 |
| 25-9T | Holly B. Parker | 904-338-3416 | 3334 Lee Rd., Gainesville, FL 37123 | $21,563,234.00 |
| 27-4Q | George F. Dorts | 615-227-1245 | 124 River Dr., Franklin, TN 29185 | $10,314,545.00 |
| 29-2D | Holly B. Parker | 904-338-3416 | 3334 Lee Rd., Gainesville, FL 37123 | $25,559,999.00 |
| 31-7P | William K. Moor | 904-445-2719 | 216 Morton Rd., Stetson, FL 30155 | $56,850,000.00 |

*Figure 1.2. Table for exercise #5, by A. Watt.*

## Attribution

This chapter of *Database Design* (including its images, unless otherwise noted) is a derivative copy of Database System Concepts by Nguyen Kim Anh licensed under Creative Commons Attribution License 3.0 license

The following material was written by Adrienne Watt:

1. Introduction
2. Key Terms
3. Exercises

# Chapter 2 Fundamental Concepts

## What Is a Database?

A *database* is a shared collection of related data used to support the activities of a particular organization. A database can be viewed as a repository of data that is defined once and then accessed by various users as shown in Figure 2.1.

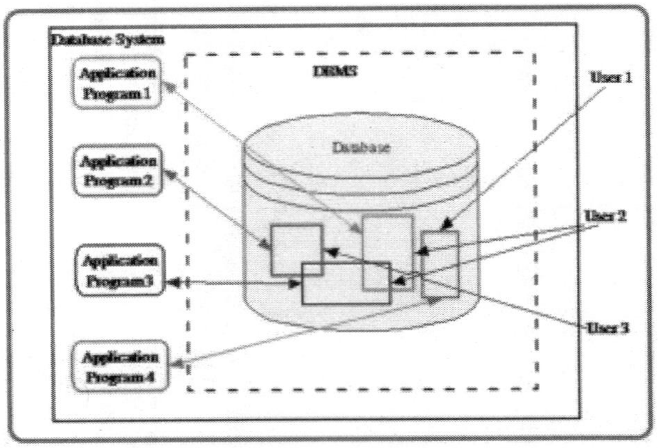


*Figure 2.1. A database is a repository of data.*

## Database Properties

A database has the following properties:

- It is a representation of some aspect of the real world or a collection of *data elements* (facts) representing real-world information.
- A database is logical, coherent and internally consistent.
- A database is designed, built and populated with data for a specific purpose.
- Each data item is stored in a field.
- A combination of fields makes up a *table*. For example, each field in an employee table contains data about an individual employee.

A database can contain many tables. For example, a membership system may contain an address table and an individual member table as shown in Figure 2.2. Members of Science World are individuals, group homes, businesses and corporations who have an active membership to Science World. Memberships can be purchased for a one- or two-year period, and then renewed for another one- or two-year period.

# Membership

ID 100755 EXPIRY DATE 201503 Prev Exp 201402 Stat A Cat FF

Name Mrs. Minnie Mouse Res 222-2222

Addres 8982 Rodent Lane

City West Vancouver Prov BC Country Canada

Notes

Cards 2013/08/09 # Members 8 #Years 1

| FirstName | LastName | YYMM | G | BARCODE | V | DATE | TIME | F |
|---|---|---|---|---|---|---|---|---|
| Mickey | Mouse | 0000 | M | 10000001 | 4 | 20130810 | 10:12:29 | y |
| Minnie | Mouse | 0000 | F | 10000002 | 4 | 20130810 | 10:12:29 | y |
| Mighty | Mouse | 0000 | M | 10000003 | 4 | 20130810 | 10:12:29 | y |
| Door | Mouse | 0000 | F | 10000004 | 4 | 20130810 | 10:12:29 | y |
| Tom | Mouse | 0000 | M | 10000005 | 4 | 20130810 | 10:12:29 | y |
| King | Rat | 0000 | M | 10000006 | 4 | 20130810 | 10:12:29 | y |
| Man | Mouse | 0000 | M | 10000007 | 4 | 20130810 | 10:12:29 | y |
| Moose | Mouse | 0000 | M | 10000008 | 4 | 20130810 | 10:12:29 | y |

Record: 1 of 1 No Filter Search

*Figure 2.2. Membership system at Science World by N. Eng.*

In Figure 2.2, Minnie Mouse renewed the family membership with Science World. Everyone with membership ID#100755 lives at 8932 Rodent Lane. The individual members are Mickey Mouse, Minnie Mouse, Mighty Mouse, Door Mouse, Tom Mouse, King Rat, Man Mouse and Moose Mouse.

## Database Management System

A *database management system* (DBMS) is a collection of programs that enables users to create and maintain databases and control all access to them. The primary goal of a DBMS is to provide an environment that is both convenient and efficient for users to retrieve and store information.

With the database approach, we can have the traditional banking system as shown in Figure 2.3. In this bank example, a DBMS is used by the Personnel Department, the Account Department and the Loan Department to access the shared corporate database.

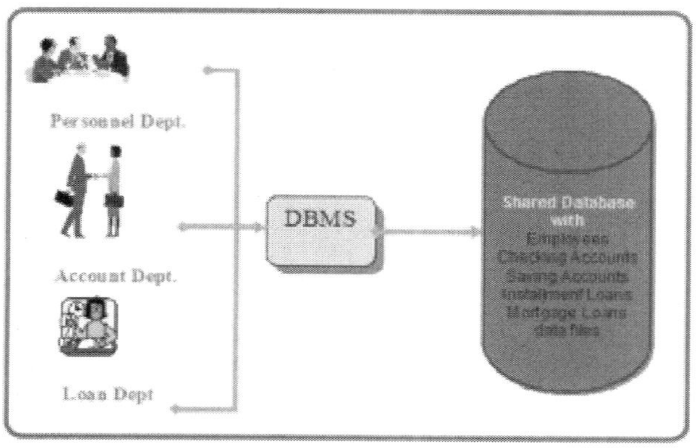


*Figure 2.3. A bank database management system (DBMS).*

Key Terms

**data elements**: facts that represent real-world information

**database**: a shared collection of related data used to support the activities of a particular organization

**database management system (DBMS)**: a collection of programs that enables users to create and maintain databases and control all access to them

**table**: a combination of fields

Exercises

1. What is a database management system (DBMS)?
2. What are the properties of a DBMS?
3. Provide three examples of a real-world database (e.g., the library contains a database of books).

## Attribution



The following material was written by Nelson Eng:

1. Example under *Database Properties*
2. Key Terms

The following material was written by Adrienne Watt:

1. Exercises

# Chapter 3 Characteristics and Benefits of a Database

Managing information means taking care of it so that it works for us and is useful for the tasks we perform. By using a DBMS, the information we collect and add to its database is no longer subject to accidental disorganization. It becomes more accessible and integrated with the rest of our work. Managing information using a database allows us to become strategic users of the data we have.

We often need to access and re-sort data for various uses. These may include:

- Creating mailing lists
- Writing management reports
- Generating lists of selected news stories
- Identifying various client needs

The processing power of a database allows it to manipulate the data it houses, so it can:

- Sort
- Match
- Link
- Aggregate
- Skip fields
- Calculate
- Arrange

Because of the versatility of databases, we find them powering all sorts of projects. A database can be linked to:

- A website that is capturing registered users
- A client-tracking application for social service organizations
- A medical record system for a health care facility
- Your personal address book in your email client
- A collection of word-processed documents
- A system that issues airline reservations

## Characteristics and Benefits of a Database

There are a number of characteristics that distinguish the database approach from the file-based system or approach. This chapter describes the benefits (and features) of the database system.

### Self-describing nature of a database system

A database system is referred to as *self-describing* because it not only contains the database itself, but also *metadata* which defines and describes the data and relationships between tables in the database. This information is used by the DBMS software or database users if needed. This separation of data and information about the data makes a database system totally different from the traditional file-based system in which the data definition is part of the application programs.

## Insulation between program and data

In the file-based system, the structure of the data files is defined in the application programs so if a user wants to change the structure of a file, all the programs that access that file might need to be changed as well.

On the other hand, in the database approach, the data structure is stored in the system catalogue and not in the programs. Therefore, one change is all that is needed to change the structure of a file. This insulation between the programs and data is also called program-data independence.

## Support for multiple views of data

A database supports multiple views of data. A *view* is a subset of the database, which is defined and dedicated for particular users of the system. Multiple users in the system might have different views of the system. Each view might contain only the data of interest to a user or group of users.

## Sharing of data and multiuser system

Current database systems are designed for multiple users. That is, they allow many users to access the same database at the same time. This access is achieved through features called *concurrency control strategies*. These strategies ensure that the data accessed are always correct and that data integrity is maintained.

The design of modern multiuser database systems is a great improvement from those in the past which restricted usage to one person at a time.

## Control of data redundancy

In the database approach, ideally, each data item is stored in only one place in the database. In some cases, data redundancy still exists to improve system performance, but such redundancy is controlled by application programming and kept to minimum by introducing as little redudancy as possible when designing the database.

## Data sharing

The integration of all the data, for an organization, within a database system has many advantages. First, it allows for data sharing among employees and others who have access to the system. Second, it gives users the ability to generate more information from a given amount of data than would be possible without the integration.

## Enforcement of integrity constraints

Database management systems must provide the ability to define and enforce certain constraints to ensure that users enter valid information and maintain data integrity. A *database constraint* is a restriction or rule that dictates what can be entered or edited in a table such as a postal code using a certain format or adding a valid city in the City field.

There are many types of database constraints. *Data type*, for example, determines the sort of data permitted in a field, for example numbers only. *Data uniqueness* such as the primary key ensures that no duplicates are entered. Constraints can be simple (field based) or complex (programming).

## Restriction of unauthorized access

Not all users of a database system will have the same accessing privileges. For example, one user might have *read-only access* (i.e., the ability to read a file but not make changes), while another might have *read and write privileges*, which is the ability to both read and modify a file. For this reason, a database management system should provide a security subsystem to create and control different types of user accounts and restrict unauthorized access.

## Data independence

Another advantage of a database management system is how it allows for data independence. In other words, the system data descriptions or data describing data (metadata) are separated from the application programs. This is possible because changes to the data structure are handled by the database management system and are not embedded in the program itself.

## Transaction processing

A database management system must include concurrency control subsystems. This feature ensures that data remains consistent and valid during transaction processing even if several users update the same information.

## Provision for multiple views of data

By its very nature, a DBMS permits many users to have access to its database either individually or simultaneously. It is not important for users to be aware of how and where the data they access is stored

## Backup and recovery facilities

Backup and recovery are methods that allow you to protect your data from loss. The database system provides a separate process, from that of a network backup, for backing up and recovering data. If a hard drive fails and the

database stored on the hard drive is not accessible, the only way to recover the database is from a backup.
If a computer system fails in the middle of a complex update process, the recovery subsystem is responsible for making sure that the database is restored to its original state. These are two more benefits of a database management system.

*Key Terms*

**concurrency control strategies**: features of a database that allow several users access to the same data item at the same time

**data type**: determines the sort of data permitted in a field, for example numbers only

**data uniqueness**: ensures that no duplicates are entered

**database constraint**: a restriction that determines what is allowed to be entered or edited in a table

**metadata**: defines and describes the data and relationshipsbetween tables in the database

**read and write privileges:** the ability to both read and modify a file

**read-only access:** the ability to read a file but not make changes

**self-describing**: a database system is referred to as self-describing because it not only contains the database itself, but also metadatawhich defines and describes the data and relationships between tables in the database

**view**: a subset of the database

*Exercises*

1. How is a DBMS distinguished from a file-based system?
2. What is data independence and why is it important?
3. What is the purpose of managing information?
4. Discuss the uses of databases in a business environment.
5. What is metadata?

## Attribution

This chapter of *Database Design* is a derivative copy of Database System Concepts by Nguyen Kim Anh licensed under Creative Commons Attribution License 3.0 license

The following material was written by Adrienne Watt:

1. Introduction

2. Key Terms
3. Exercises

# Chapter 4 Types of Data Models

## High-level Conceptual Data Models

High-level conceptual data models provide concepts for presenting data in ways that are close to the way people perceive data. A typical example is the entity relationship model, which uses main concepts like entities, attributes and relationships. An entity represents a real-world object such as an employee or a project. The entity has attributes that represent properties such as an employee's name, address and birthdate. A relationship represents an association among entities; for example, an employee works on many projects. A relationship exists between the employee and each project.

## Record-based Logical Data Models

Record-based logical data models provide concepts users can understand but are not too far from the way data is stored in the computer. Three well-known data models of this type are relational data models, network data models and hierarchical data models.

- The *relational model* represents data as *relations*, or tables. For example, in the membership system at Science World, each membership has many members (see Figure 2.2 in Chapter 2). The membership identifier, expiry date and address information are fields in the membership. The members are individuals such as Mickey, Minnie, Mighty, Door, Tom, King, Man and Moose. Each record is said to be an *instance* of the membership table.
- The *network model* represents data as record types. This model also represents a limited type of one to many relationship called a *set type*, as shown in Figure 4.1.

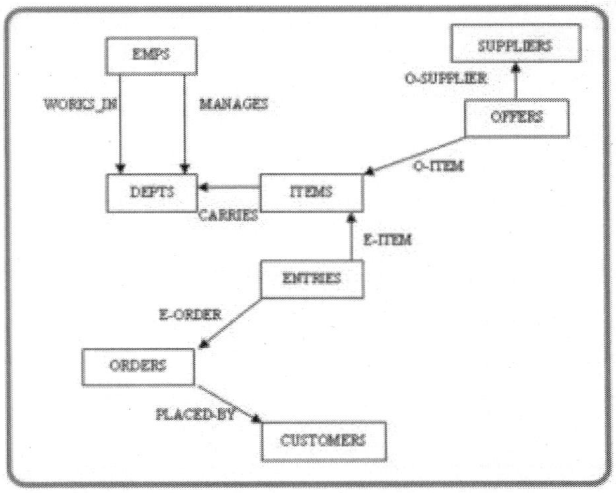


*Figure 4.1. Network model diagram.*

- The *hierarchical model* represents data as a hierarchical tree structure. Each branch of the hierarchy represents a number of related records. Figure 4.2 shows this schema in hierarchical model notation.

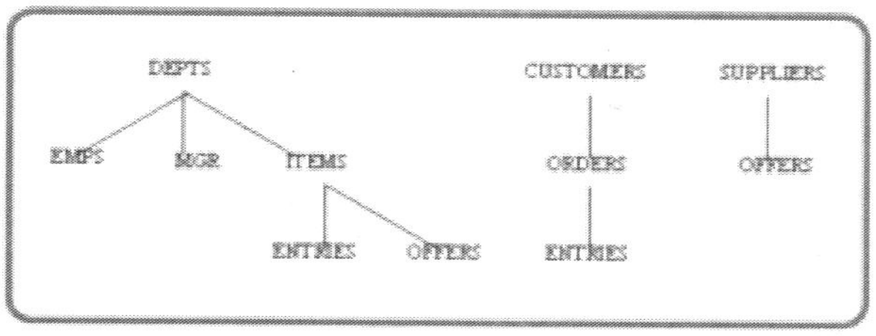


*Figure 4.2. Hierarchical model diagram.*

*Key Terms*

**hierarchical model**: represents data as a hierarchical tree structure
**instance**: a record within a table

**network model**: represents data as record types

**relation**: another term for table

**relational model**: represents data as relations or tables

**set type**: a limited type of one to many relationship

*Exercises*

1. What is a data model?
2. What is a high-level conceptual data model?
3. What is an entity? An attribute? A relationship?
4. List and briefly describe the common record-based logical data models.

## Attribution



The following material was written by Adrienne Watt:

1. Key Terms
2. Exercises

# Chapter 5 Data Modelling

*Data modelling* is the first step in the process of database design. This step is sometimes considered to be a high-level and abstract design phase, also referred to as conceptual design. The aim of this phase is to describe:

- The data contained in the database (e.g., entities: students, lecturers, courses, subjects)
- The relationships between data items (e.g., students are supervised by lecturers; lecturers teach courses)
- The constraints on data (e.g., student number has exactly eight digits; a subject has four or six units of credit only)

In the second step, the data items, the relationships and the constraints are all expressed using the concepts provided by the high-level data model. Because these concmepts do not include the implementation details, the result of the data modelling process is a (semi) formal representation of the database structure. This result is quite easy to understand so it is used as reference to make sure that all the user's requirements are met.

The third step is database design. During this step, we might have two sub-steps: one called *database logical design*, which defines a database in a data model of a specific DBMS, and another called *database physical design*, which defines the internal database storage structure, file organization or indexing techniques. These two sub-steps are database implementation and operations/user interfaces building steps.

In the database design phases, data are represented using a certain data model. The *data model* is a collection of concepts or notations for describing data, data relationships, data semantics and data constraints. Most data models also include a set of basic operations for manipulating data in the database.

## Degrees of Data Abstraction

In this section we will look at the database design process in terms of specificity. Just as any design starts at a high level and proceeds to an ever-increasing level of detail, so does database design. For example, when building a home, you start with how many bedrooms and bathrooms the home will have, whether it will be on one level or multiple levels, etc. The next step is to get an architect to design the home from a more structured perspective. This level gets more detailed with respect to actual room sizes, how the home will be wired, where the plumbing fixtures will be placed, etc. The last step is to hire a contractor to build the home. That's looking at the design from a high level of abstraction to an increasing level of detail.

The database design is very much like that. It starts with users identifying the business rules; then the database designers and analysts create the database design; and then the database administrator implements the design using a DBMS.

The following subsections summarize the models in order of decreasing level of abstraction.

### External models

- Represent the user's view of the database
- Contain multiple different external views

- Are closely related to the real world as perceived by each user

## Conceptual models

- Provide flexible data-structuring capabilities
- Present a "community view": the logical structure of the entire database
- Contain data stored in the database
- Show relationships among data including:
    - Constraints
    - Semantic information (e.g., business rules)
    - Security and integrity information
- Consider a database as a collection of entities (objects) of various kinds
- Are the basis for identification and high-level description of main data objects; they avoid details
- Are database independent regardless of the database you will be using

## Internal models

The three best-known models of this kind are the relational data model, the network data model and the hierarchical data model. These internal models:

- Consider a database as a collection of fixed-size records
- Are closer to the physical level or file structure
- Are a representation of the database as seen by the DBMS.
- Require the designer to match the conceptual model's characteristics and constraints to those of the selected implementation model
- Involve mapping the entities in the conceptual model to the tables in the relational model

## Physical models

- Are the physical representation of the database
- Have the lowest level of abstractions
- Are how the data is stored; they deal with
    - Run-time performance
    - Storage utilization and compression
    - File organization and access methods
    - Data encryption
- Are the physical level – managed by the *operating system* (OS)
- Provide concepts that describe the details of how data are stored in the computer's memory

## Data Abstraction Layer

In a pictorial view, you can see how the different models work together. Let's look at this from the highest level, the external model.

The external model is the end user's view of the data. Typically a database is an enterprise system that serves the needs of multiple departments. However, one department is not interested in seeing other departments' data (e.g., the human resources (HR) department does not care to view the sales department's data). Therefore, one user view will differ from another.

The external model requires that the designer subdivide a set of requirements and constraints into functional modules that can be examined within the framework of their external models (e.g., human resources versus sales).

As a data designer, you need to understand all the data so that you can build an enterprise-wide database. Based on the needs of various departments, the conceptual model is the first model created.

At this stage, the conceptual model is independent of both software and hardware. It does not depend on the DBMS software used to implement the model. It does not depend on the hardware used in the implementation of the model. Changes in either hardware or DBMS software have no effect on the database design at the conceptual level.

Once a DBMS is selected, you can then implement it. This is the internal model. Here you create all the tables, constraints, keys, rules, etc. This is often referred to as the *logical design*.

The physical model is simply the way the data is stored on disk. Each database vendor has its own way of storing the data.

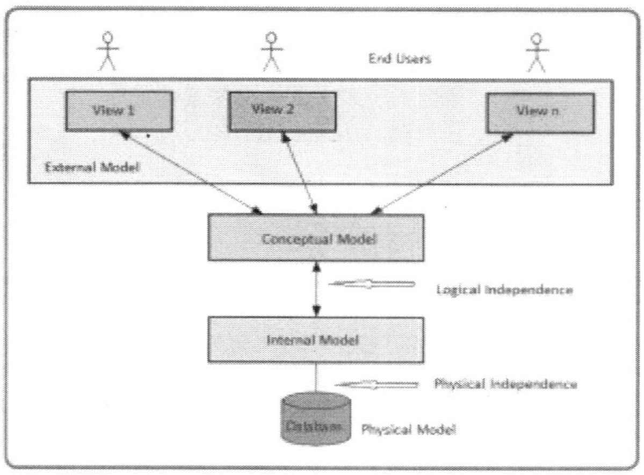


*Figure 5.1. Data abstraction layers.*

## Schemas

A *schema* is an overall description of a database, and it is usually represented by the *entity relationship diagram* (ERD). There are many subschemas that represent external models and thus display external views of the data. Below is a list of items to consider during the design process of a database.

- External schemas: there are multiple

- Multiple subschemas: these display multiple external views of the data
- Conceptual schema: there is only one. This schema includes data items, relationships and constraints, all represented in an ERD.
- Physical schema: there is only one

## Logical and Physical Data Independence

*Data independence* refers to the immunity of user applications to changes made in the definition and organization of data. Data abstractions expose only those items that are important or pertinent to the user. Complexity is hidden from the database user.

Data independence and operation independence together form the feature of data abstraction. There are two types of data independence: logical and physical.

### Logical data independence

A *logical schema* is a conceptual design of the database done on paper or a whiteboard, much like architectural drawings for a house. The ability to change the logical schema, without changing the *external schema* or user view, is called *logical data independence*. For example, the addition or removal of new entities, attributes or relationships to this *conceptual schema* should be possible without having to change existing external schemas or rewrite existing application programs.

In other words, changes to the logical schema (e.g., alterations to the structure of the database like adding a column or other tables) should not affect the function of the application (external views).

### Physical data independence

*Physical data independence* refers to the immunity of the internal model to changes in the physical model. The logical schema stays unchanged even though changes are made to file organization or storage structures, storage devices or indexing strategy.

Physical data independence deals with hiding the details of the storage structure from user applications. The applications should not be involved with these issues, since there is no difference in the operation carried out against the data.

*Key Terms*

**conceptual model**: the logical structure of the entire database
**conceptual schema**: another term for logical schema

**data independence**: the immunity of user applications to changes made in the definition and organization of data

**data model**:a collection of concepts or notations for describing data, data relationships, data semantics and data constraints

**data modelling**: the first step in the process of database design

**database logical design**: defines a database in a data model of a specific database management system

**database physical design:** defines the internal database storage structure, file organization or indexing techniques

**entity relationship diagram (ERD)**: a data model describing the database showing tables, attributes and relationships

**external model**: represents the user's view of the database

**external schema**: user view

**internal model:** a representation of the database as seen by the DBMS

**logical data independence**: the ability to change the logical schema without changing the external schema

**logical design**: where you create all the tables, constraints, keys, rules, etc.

**logical schema**: a conceptual design of the database done on paper or a whiteboard, much like architectural drawings for a house

**operating system (OS)**: manages the physical level of the physical model

**physical data independence**: the immunity of the internal model to changes in the physical model

**physical model**: the physical representation of the database

**schema**: an overall description of a database

*Exercises*

1. Describe the purpose of a conceptual design.
2. How is a conceptual design different from a logical design?
3. What is an external model?
4. What is a conceptual model?
5. What is an internal model?
6. What is a physical model?
7. Which model does the database administrator work with?
8. Which model does the end user work with?
9. What is logical data independence?
10. What is physical data independence?

Also see *Appendix A: University Registration Data Model Example*

## Attribution

This chapter of *Database Design* is a derivative copy of Database System Concepts by Nguyen Kim Anh licensed under Creative Commons Attribution License 3.0 license

The following material was written by Adrienne Watt:

1. Some or all of the introduction, degrees of data abstraction, data abstraction layer
2. Key Terms
3. Exercises

# Chapter 6 Classification of Database Management Systems

Database management systems can be classified based on several criteria, such as the data model, user numbers and database distribution, all described below.

## Classification Based on Data Model

The most popular data model in use today is the relational data model. Well-known DBMSs like Oracle, MS SQL Server, DB2 and MySQL support this model. Other traditional models, such as hierarchical data models and network data models, are still used in industry mainly on mainframe platforms. However, they are not commonly used due to their complexity. These are all referred to as *traditional models* because they preceded the relational model.

In recent years, the newer *object-oriented data models* were introduced. This model is a database management system in which information is represented in the form of objects as used in object-oriented programming. Object-oriented databases are different from relational databases, which are table-oriented. Object-oriented database management systems (OODBMS) combine database capabilities with object-oriented programming language capabilities.

The object-oriented models have not caught on as expected so are not in widespread use. Some examples of object-oriented DBMSs are O2, ObjectStore and Jasmine.

## Classification Based on User Numbers

A DBMS can be classification based on the number of users it supports. It can be a *single-user database system*, which supports one user at a time, or a *multiuser database system*, which supports multiple users concurrently.

## Classification Based on Database Distribution

There are four main distribution systems for database systems and these, in turn, can be used to classify the DBMS.

### Centralized systems

With a *centralized database system*, the DBMS and database are stored at a single site that is used by several other systems too. This is illustrated in Figure 6.1.

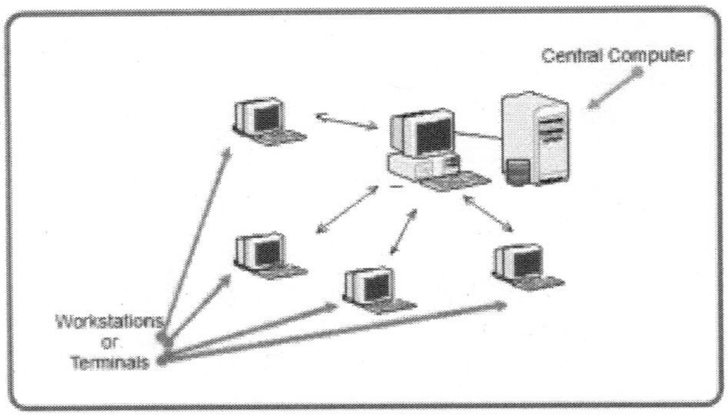


*Figure 6.1. Example of a centralized database system.*

In the early 1980s, many Canadian libraries used the GEAC 8000 to convert their manual card catalogues to machine-readable centralized catalogue systems. Each book catalogue had a barcode field similar to those on supermarket products.

## Distributed database system

In a *distributed database system*, the actual database and the DBMS software are distributed from various sites that are connected by a computer network, as shown in Figure 6.2.

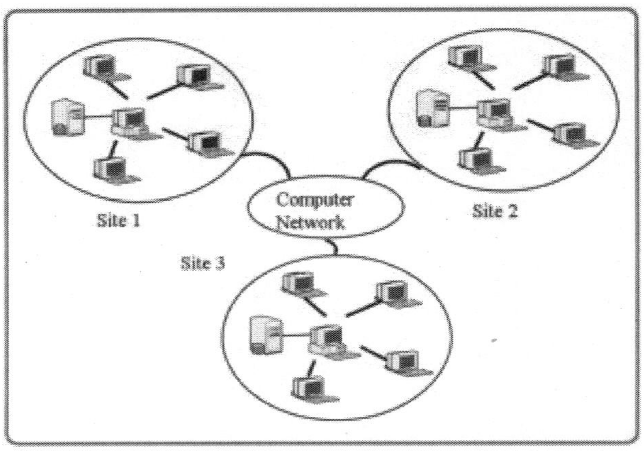


*Figure 6.2. Example of a distributed database system.*

## Homogeneous distributed database systems

*Homogeneous distributed database systems* use the same DBMS software from multiple sites. Data exchange between these various sites can be handled easily. For example, library information systems by the same vendor, such as Geac Computer Corporation, use the same DBMS software which allows easy data exchange between the various Geac library sites.

## Heterogeneous distributed database systems

In a *heterogeneous distributed database system*, different sites might use different DBMS software, but there is additional common software to support data exchange between these sites. For example, the various library database systems use the same machine-readable cataloguing (MARC) format to support library record data exchange.

*Key Terms*

**centralized database system:** the DBMS and database are stored at a single site that is used by several other systems too

**distributed database system**: the actual database and the DBMS software are distributed from various sites that are connected by a computer network

**heterogeneous distributed database system**: different sites might use different DBMS software, but there is additional common software to support data exchange between these sites

**homogeneous distributed database systems**: use the same DBMS software at multiple sites

**multiuser database system**: a database management system which supports multiple users concurrently

**object-oriented data model**: a database management system in which information is represented in the form of objects as used in object-oriented programming

**single-user database system**: a database management system which supports one user at a time

**traditional models**: data models that preceded the relational model

*Exercises*

1. Provide three examples of the most popular relational databases used.
2. What is the difference between centralized and distributed database systems?
3. What is the difference between homogenous distributed database systems and heterogeneous distributed database systems?

## Attribution



The following material was written by Adrienne Watt:

1. Key Terms
2. Exercises

# Chapter 7 The Relational Data Model

The relational data model was introduced by E. F. Codd in 1970. Currently, it is the most widely used data model.

The relational model has provided the basis for:

- Research on the theory of data/relationship/constraint
- Numerous database design methodologies
- The standard database access language called *structured query language* (SQL)
- Almost all modern commercial database management systems

The relational data model describes the world as "a collection of inter-related relations (or tables)."

## Fundamental Concepts in the Relational Data Model

### Relation

A *relation*, also known as a *table* or *file*, is a subset of the Cartesian product of a list of domains characterized by a name. And within a table, each row represents a group of related data values. A *row*, or record, is also known as a *tuple*. The columns in a table is a field and is also referred to as an attribute. You can also think of it this way: an attribute is used to define the record and a record contains a set of attributes.

The steps below outline the logic between a relation and its domains.

1. Given *n* domains are denoted by D1, D2, ... Dn
2. And *r* is a relation defined on these domains
3. Then $r \subseteq D1 \times D2 \times \ldots \times Dn$

### Table

A database is composed of multiple tables and each table holds the data. Figure 7.1 shows a database that contains three tables.

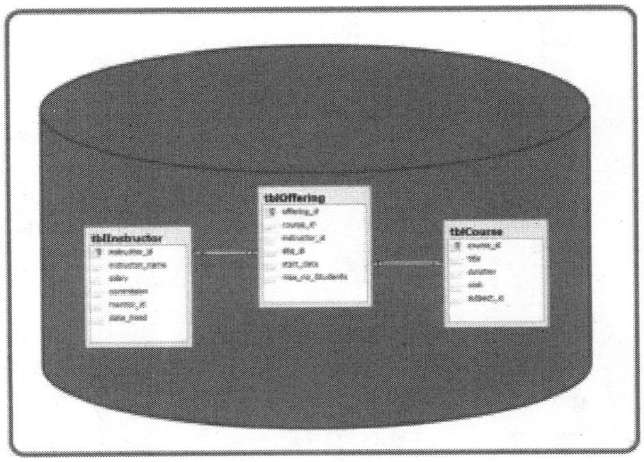


*Figure 7.1. Database with three tables.*

## Column

A database stores pieces of information or facts in an organized way. Understanding how to use and get the most out of databases requires us to understand that method of organization.

The principal storage units are called *columns* or *fields* or *attributes*. These house the basic components of data into which your content can be broken down. When deciding which fields to create, you need to think generically about your information, for example, drawing out the common components of the information that you will store in the database and avoiding the specifics that distinguish one item from another.

Look at the example of an ID card in Figure 7.2 to see the relationship between fields and their data.

| Field Name | Data |
|---|---|
| First Name | Isabelle |
| Family Name | Whelan |
| Nationality | British |
| Salary | 109,900 |
| Date of Birth | 15 September 1983 |
| Marital Status | Single |
| Shift | Mon, Wed |
| Place of issue | Addis Ababa |
| Valid until | 17 December 2003 |

*Figure 7.2. Example of an ID card by A. Watt.*

## Domain

A *domain* is the original sets of atomic values used to model data. By *atomic value*, we mean that each value in the domain is indivisible as far as the relational model is concerned. For example:

- The domain of Marital Status has a set of possibilities: Married, Single, Divorced.
- The domain of Shift has the set of all possible days: {Mon, Tue, Wed…}.

- The domain of Salary is the set of all floating-point numbers greater than 0 and less than 200,000.
- The domain of First Name is the set of character strings that represents names of people.

In summary, a domain is a set of acceptable values that a column is allowed to contain. This is based on various properties and the data type for the column. We will discuss data types in another chapter.

## Records

Just as the content of any one document or item needs to be broken down into its constituent bits of data for storage in the fields, the link between them also needs to be available so that they can be reconstituted into their whole form. Records allow us to do this. *Records* contain fields that are related, such as a customer or an employee. As noted earlier, a tuple is another term used for record.

Records and fields form the basis of all databases. A simple table  gives us the clearest picture of how records and fields work together in a database storage project.

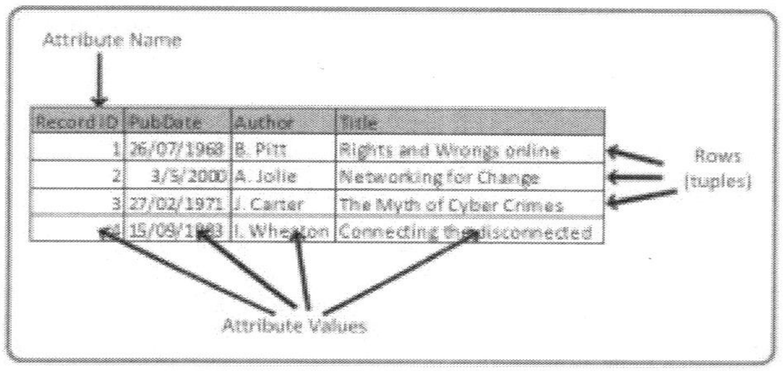


*Figure 7.3. Example of a simple table by A. Watt.*

The simple table example in Figure 7.3 shows us how fields can hold a range of different sorts of data. This one has:

- A Record ID field: this is an ordinal number; its data type is an integer.
- A PubDate field: this is displayed as day/month/year; its data type is date.
- An Author field: this is displayed as Initial. Surname; its data type is text.
- A Title field text: free text can be entered here.

You can command the database to sift through its data and organize it in a particular way. For example, you can request that a selection of records be limited by date: 1. all before a given date, 2. all after a given date or 3. all between two given dates. Similarly, you can choose to have records sorted by date. Because the field, or record, containing the data is set up as a Date field, the database reads the information in the Date field not just as numbers separated by slashes, but rather, as dates that must be ordered according to a calendar system.

## Degree

The *degree* is the number of attributes in a table. In our example in Figure 7.3, the degree is 4.

## Properties of a Table

- A table has a name that is distinct from all other tables in the database.
- There are no duplicate rows; each row is distinct.
- Entries in columns are atomic. The table does not contain repeating groups or multivalued attributes.
- Entries from columns are from the same domain based on their data type including:
  - number (numeric, integer, float, smallint,...)
  - character (string)
  - date
  - logical (true or false)
- Operations combining different data types are disallowed.
- Each attribute has a distinct name.
- The sequence of columns is insignificant.
- The sequence of rows is insignificant.

*Key Terms*

**atomic value**: each value in the domain is indivisible as far as the relational model is concerned**attribute**: principle storage unit in a database

**column:** see *attribute*

**degree**: number of attributes in a table

**domain**: the original sets of atomic values used to model data; a set of acceptable values that a column is allowed to contain

**field**: see *attribute*

**file**:see *relation*

**record**: contains fields that are related; *see tuple*

**relation**: a subset of the Cartesian product of a list of domains characterized by a name; the technical term for table or file

**row**: *see tuple*

**structured query language (SQL)**: the standard database access language

**table**:see *relation*

**tuple**: a technical term for row or record

## *Terminology Key*

Several of the terms used in this chapter are synonymous. In addition to the Key Terms above, please refer to Table 7.1 below. The terms in the Alternative 1 column are most commonly used.

| Formal Terms (Codd) | Alternative 1 | Alternative 2 |
|---|---|---|
| Relation | Table | File |
| Tuple | Row | Record |
| Attribute | Column | Field |

*Table 7.1. Terms and their synonyms by A. Watt.*

## *Exercises*

*Use Table 7.2 to answer questions 1–4.*

1. Using correct terminology, identify and describe all the components in Table 7.2.
2. What is the possible domain for field EmpJobCode?
3. How many records are shown?
4. How many attributes are shown?
5. List the properties of a table.

**EMPLOYEE**

| EMPID | EMPLNAME | EMPINIT | EMPFNAME | EMPJOBCODE |
|---|---|---|---|---|
| 123455 | Friedman | A. | Robert | 12 |
| 123456 | Olanski | D. | Delbert | 18 |
| 123457 | Fontein | G. | Juliette | 15 |
| 123458 | Cruazona | X. | Maria | 18 |

*Table 7.2. Table for exercise questions, by A. Watt.*

## Attribution

This chapter of *Database Design* (including images, except as otherwise noted) is a derivative copy of Relational Design Theory by Nguyen Kim Anh licensed under Creative Commons Attribution License 3.0 license

The following material was written by Adrienne Watt:

1. All or part of the sections on relations, tables, columns and degree
2. Key Terms
3. Exercises

# Chapter 8 The Entity Relationship Data Model

The *entity relationship* (ER) *data model* has existed for over 35 years. It is well suited to data modelling for use with databases because it is fairly abstract and is easy to discuss and explain. ER models are readily translated to relations. ER models, also called an ER schema, are represented by ER diagrams.

ER modelling is based on two concepts:

- Entities, defined as tables that hold specific information (data)
- *Relationships*, defined as the associations or interactions between entities

Here is an example of how these two concepts might be combined in an ER data model: Prof. Ba (entity) teaches (relationship) the Database Systems course (entity).

For the rest of this chapter, we will use a sample database called the COMPANY database to illustrate the concepts of the ER model. This database contains information about employees, departments and projects. Important points to note include:

- There are several departments in the company. Each department has a unique identification, a name, location of the office and a particular employee who manages the department.
- A department controls a number of projects, each of which has a unique name, a unique number and a budget.
- Each employee has a name, identification number, address, salary and birthdate. An employee is assigned to one department but can join in several projects. We need to record the start date of the employee in each project. We also need to know the direct supervisor of each employee.
- We want to keep track of the dependents for each employee. Each dependent has a name, birthdate and relationship with the employee.

## Entity, Entity Set and Entity Type

An *entity* is an object in the real world with an independent existence that can be differentiated from other objects. An entity might be

- An object with physical existence (e.g., a lecturer, a student, a car)
- An object with conceptual existence (e.g., a course, a job, a position)

Entities can be classified based on their strength. An entity is considered weak if its tables are existence dependent.

- That is, it cannot exist without a relationship with another entity
- Its primary key is derived from the primary key of the parent entity
    - The Spouse table, in the COMPANY database, is a weak entity because its primary key is dependent on the Employee table. Without a corresponding employee record, the spouse record would not exist.

An entity is considered strong if it can exist apart from all of its related entities.

- Kernels are strong entities.
- A table without a foreign key or a table that contains a foreign key that can contain nulls is a strong entity

Another term to know is *entity type* which defines a collection of similar entities.

An *entity set* is a collection of entities of an entity type at a particular point of time. In an entity relationship diagram (ERD), an entity type is represented by a name in a box. For example, in Figure 8.1, the entity type is EMPLOYEE.

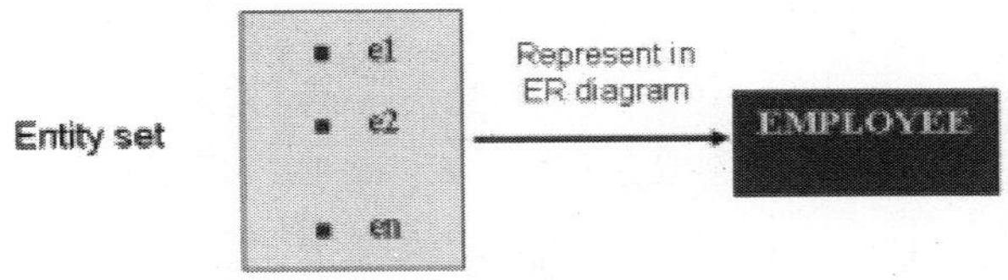


*Figure* 8.1. ERD *with entity type* EMPLOYEE.

## Existence dependency

An entity's existence is dependent on the existence of the related entity. It is existence-dependent if it has a mandatory foreign key (i.e., a foreign key attribute that cannot be null). For example, in the COMPANY database, a Spouse entity is existence -dependent on the Employee entity.

## Kinds of Entities

You should also be familiar with different kinds of entities including independent entities, dependent entities and characteristic entities. These are described below.

## Independent entities

*Independent entities*, also referred to as kernels, are the backbone of the database. They are what other tables are based on. *Kernels* have the following characteristics:

- They are the building blocks of a database.
- The primary key may be simple or composite.
- The primary key is not a foreign key.
- They do not depend on another entity for their existence.

If we refer back to our COMPANY database, examples of an independent entity include the Customer table, Employee table or Product table.

## Dependent entities

*Dependent entities*, also referred to as *derived entities*, depend on other tables for their meaning. These entities have the following characteristics:

- Dependent entities are used to connect two kernels together.
- They are said to be existence dependent on two or more tables.
- Many to many relationships become associative tables with at least two foreign keys.
- They may contain other attributes.
- The foreign key identifies each associated table.
- There are three options for the primary key:

1. Use a composite of foreign keys of associated tables if unique
2. Use a composite of foreign keys and a qualifying column
3. Create a new simple primary key

## Characteristic entities

*Characteristic entities* provide more information about another table. These entities have the following characteristics:

- They represent multivalued attributes.
- They describe other entities.
- They typically have a one to many relationship.
- The foreign key is used to further identify the characterized table.
- Options for primary key are as follows:

1. Use a composite of foreign key plus a qualifying column
2. Create a new simple primary key. In the COMPANY database, these might include:
   - Employee (EID, Name, Address, Age, Salary) – EID is the simple primary key.
   - EmployeePhone (EID, Phone) – EID is part of a composite primary key. Here, EID is also a foreign key.

# Attributes

Each entity is described by a set of attributes (e.g., Employee = (Name, Address, Birthdate (Age), Salary).

Each attribute has a name, and is associated with an entity and a domain of legal values. However, the information about attribute domain is not presented on the ERD.

In the entity relationship diagram, shown in Figure 8.2, each attribute is represented by an oval with a name inside.

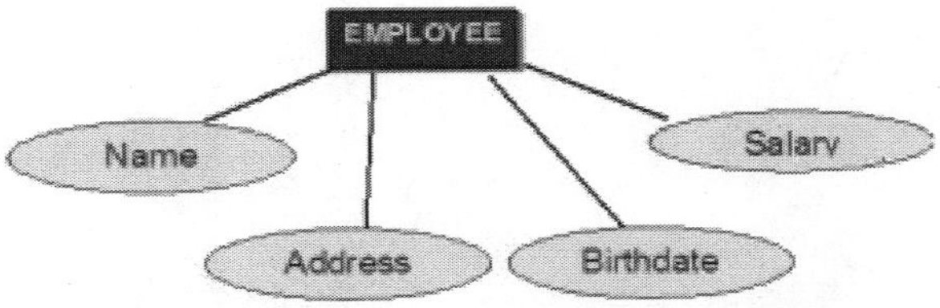


*Figure 8.2. How attributes are represented in an ERD.*

## Types of Attributes

There are a few types of attributes you need to be familiar with. Some of these are to be left as is, but some need to be adjusted to facilitate representation in the relational model. This first section will discuss the types of attributes. Later on we will discuss fixing the attributes to fit correctly into the relational model.

### Simple attributes

*Simple attributes* are those drawn from the atomic value domains; they are also called *single-valued attributes.* In the COMPANY database, an example of this would be: Name = {John} ; Age = {23}

### Composite attributes

*Composite attributes* are those that consist of a hierarchy of attributes. Using our database example, and shown in Figure 8.3, Address may consist of Number, Street and Suburb. So this would be written as → Address = {59 + 'Meek Street' + 'Kingsford'}

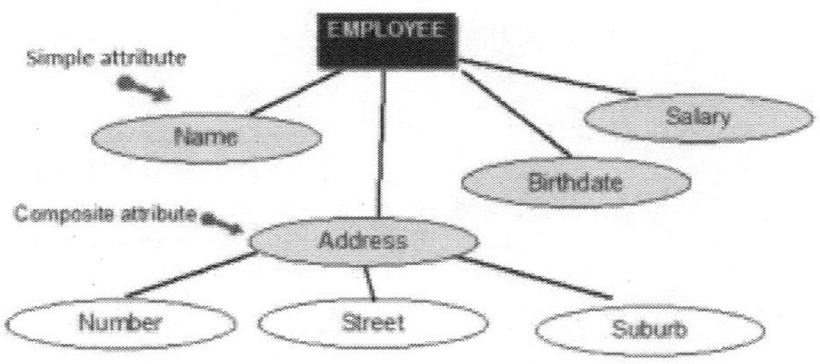


*Figure 8.3. An example of composite attributes.*

### Multivalued attributes

*Multivalued attributes* are attributes that have a set of values for each entity. An example of a multivalued attribute from the COMPANY database, as seen in Figure 8.4, are the degrees of an employee: BSc, MIT, PhD.

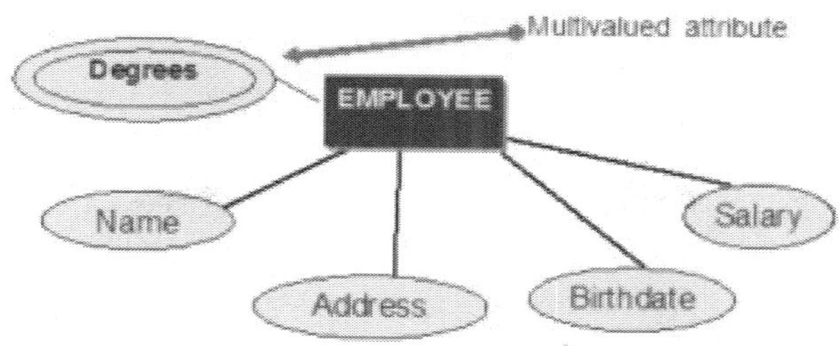

*Figure 8.4. Example of a multivalued attribute.*

## Derived attributes

*Derived attributes* are attributes that contain values calculated from other attributes. An example of this can be seen in Figure 8.5. Age can be derived from the attribute Birthdate. In this situation, Birthdate is called a *stored attribute*, which is physically saved to the database.

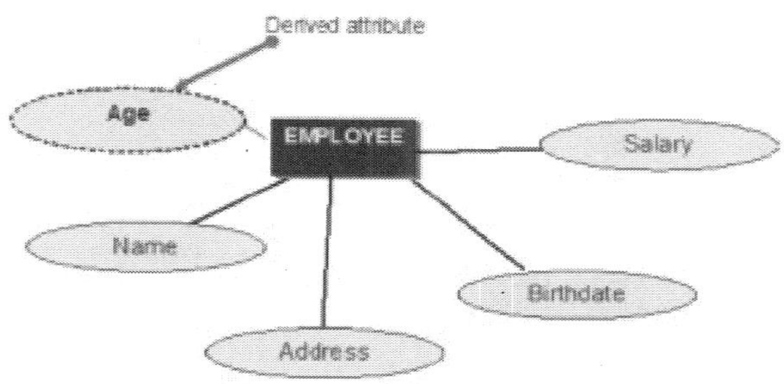

*Figure 8.5. Example of a derived attribute.*

# Keys

An important constraint on an entity is the key. The *key* is an attribute or a group of attributes whose values can be used to uniquely identify an individual entity in an entity set.

# Types of Keys

There are several types of keys. These are described below.

## Candidate key

A *candidate key* is a simple or composite key that is unique and minimal. It is unique because no two rows in a table may have the same value at any time. It is minimal because every column is necessary in order to attain uniqueness.

From our COMPANY database example, if the entity is **Employee**(EID, First Name, Last Name, SIN, Address, Phone, BirthDate, Salary, DepartmentID), possible candidate keys are:

- EID, SIN
- First Name and Last Name – assuming there is no one else in the company with the same name
- Last Name and DepartmentID – assuming two people with the same last name don't work in the same department

## Composite key

A *composite key* is composed of two or more attributes, but it must be minimal.

Using the example from the candidate key section, possible composite keys are:

- First Name and Last Name – assuming there is no one else in the company with the same name
- Last Name and Department ID – assuming two people with the same last name don't work in the same department

## Primary key

The primary key is a candidate key that is selected by the database designer to be used as an identifying mechanism for the whole entity set. It must uniquely identify tuples in a table and not be null. The primary key is indicated in the ER model by underlining the attribute.

- A candidate key is selected by the designer to uniquely identify tuples in a table. It must not be null.
- A key is chosen by the database designer to be used as an identifying mechanism for the whole entity set. This is referred to as the primary key. This key is indicated by underlining the attribute in the ER model.

In the following example, EID is the primary key:

**Employee**(<u>EID</u>, First Name, Last Name, SIN, Address, Phone, BirthDate, Salary, DepartmentID)

## Secondary key

A *secondary key* is an attribute used strictly for retrieval purposes (can be composite), for example: Phone and Last Name.

## Alternate key

*Alternate keys* are all candidate keys not chosen as the primary key.

## Foreign key

A *foreign key* (FK) is an attribute in a table that references the primary key in another table OR it can be null. Both foreign and primary keys must be of the same data type.

In the COMPANY database example below, DepartmentID is the foreign key:

**Employee**(EID, First Name, Last Name, SIN, Address, Phone, BirthDate, Salary, DepartmentID)

# Nulls

A *null* is a special symbol, independent of data type, which means either unknown or inapplicable. It does not mean zero or blank. Features of null include:

- No data entry
- Not permitted in the primary key
- Should be avoided in other attributes
- Can represent
    - An unknown attribute value
    - A known, but missing, attribute value
    - A “not applicable” condition
- Can create problems when functions such as COUNT, AVERAGE and SUM are used
- Can create logical problems when relational tables are linked

NOTE: The result of a comparison operation is null when either argument is null. The result of an arithmetic operation is null when either argument is null (except functions that ignore nulls).

## Example of how null can be used

Use the Salary table (Salary_tbl) in Figure 8.6 to follow an example of how null can be used.

**Salary_tbl**

| emp# | jobName | salary | commission |
|---|---|---|---|
| E10 | Sales | 12500 | 32090 |
| E11 | Null | 25000 | 8000 |
| E12 | Sales | 44000 | 0 |
| E13 | Sales | 44000 | Null |

*Figure 8.6. Salary table for null example, by* A. Watt.

To begin, find all employees (emp#) in Sales (under the jobName column) whose salary plus commission are greater than 30,000.

- SELECT emp# FROM Salary_tbl
- WHERE jobName = Sales AND
- (commission + salary) > 30,000 –> E10 and E12

This result does not include E13 because of the null value in the commission column. To ensure that the row with the null value is included, we need to look at the individual fields. By adding commission and salary for employee E13, the result will be a null value. The solution is shown below.

- SELECT emp# FROM Salary_tbl
- WHERE jobName = Sales AND
- (commission > 30000 OR
- salary > 30000 OR
- (commission + salary) > 30,000 –>E10 and E12 and E13

## Relationships

*Relationships* are the glue that holds the tables together. They are used to connect related information between tables.

*Relationship strength* is based on how the primary key of a related entity is defined. A weak, or non-identifying, relationship exists if the primary key of the related entity does not contain a primary key component of the parent entity. Company database examples include:

- Customer(**CustID**, CustName)
- Order(**OrderID**, CustID, Date)

A strong, or identifying, relationship exists when the primary key of the related entity contains the primary key component of the parent entity. Examples include:

- Course(**CrsCode**, DeptCode, Description)
- Class(**CrsCode, Section**, ClassTime…)

## Types of Relationships

Below are descriptions of the various types of relationships.

### One to many (1:M) relationship

A one to many (1:M) relationship should be the norm in any relational database design and is found in all relational database environments. For example, one department has many employees. Figure 8.7 shows the relationship of one of these employees to the department.

Relational Schema

EMPLOYEE(EID, Name, Address, Birthdate, Salary, DeptId)

DEPARTMENT(DeptId, Name, Office)

*Figure 8.7. Example of a one to many relationship.*

## One to one (1:1) relationship

A one to one (1:1) relationship is the relationship of one entity to only one other entity, and vice versa. It should be rare in any relational database design. In fact, it could indicate that two entities actually belong in the same table.

An example from the COMPANY database is one employee is associated with one spouse, and one spouse is associated with one employee.

## Many to many (M:N) relationships

For a many to many relationship, consider the following points:

- It cannot be implemented as such in the relational model.
- It can be changed into two 1:M relationships.
- It can be implemented by breaking up to produce a set of 1:M relationships.
- It involves the implementation of a composite entity.
- Creates two or more 1:M relationships.
- The composite entity table must contain at least the primary keys of the original tables.
- The linking table contains multiple occurrences of the foreign key values.
- Additional attributes may be assigned as needed.
- It can avoid problems inherent in an M:N relationship by creating a composite entity or bridge entity. For example, an employee can work on many projects OR a project can have many employees working on it, depending on the business rules. Or, a student can have many classes and a class can hold many students.

Figure 8.8 shows another another aspect of the M:N relationship where an employee has different start dates for different projects. Therefore, we need a JOIN table that contains the EID, Code and StartDate.

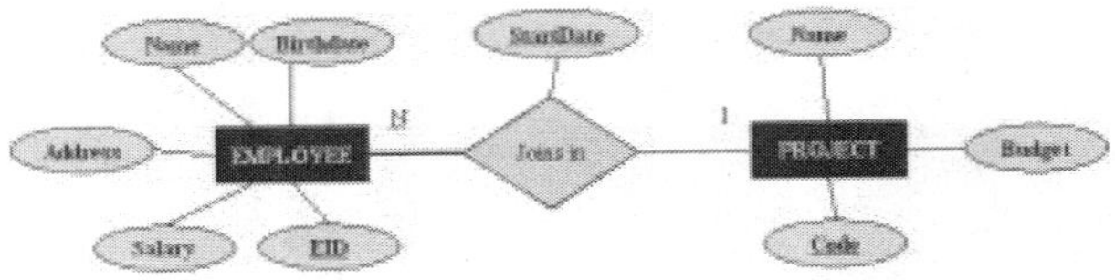


Relational Schema

EMPLOYEE (EID, Name, Address, Birthdate, Salary)

PROJECT (Code, Name, Budget)

JOIN(EID, Code, StartDate)

*Figure 8.8. Example where employee has different start dates for different projects.*

**Example of mapping an M:N binary relationship type**

- For each M:N binary relationship, identify two relations.
- A and B represent two entity types participating in R.
- Create a new relation S to represent R.
- S needs to contain the PKs of A and B. These together can be the PK in the S table OR these together with another simple attribute in the new table R can be the PK.
- The combination of the primary keys (A and B) will make the primary key of S.

## Unary relationship (recursive)

A *unary relationship*, also called *recursive*, is one in which a relationship exists between occurrences of the same entity set. In this relationship, the primary and foreign keys are the same, but they represent two entities with different roles. See Figure 8.9 for an example.

For some entities in a unary relationship, a separate column can be created that refers to the primary key of the same entity set.

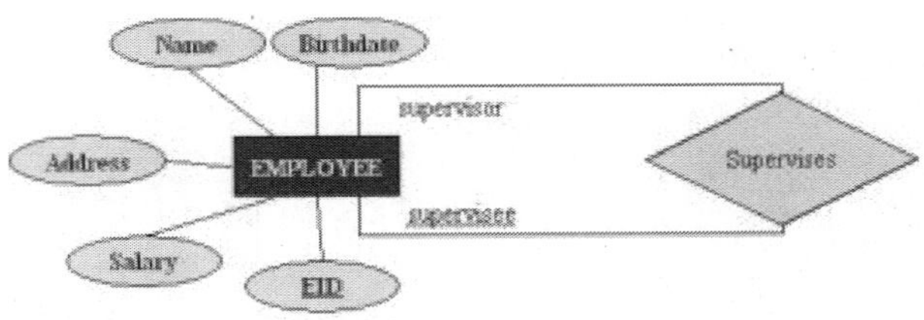


Relational Schema

EMPLOYEE (EID, Name, Address, Birthdate, Salary, *Super-EID*)

*Figure 8.9. Example of a unary relationship.*

## Ternary Relationships

A *ternary relationship* is a relationship type that involves many to many relationships between three tables.

Refer to Figure 8.10 for an example of mapping a ternary relationship type. Note *n-ary* means multiple tables in a relationship. (Remember, N = many.)

- For each n-ary (> 2) relationship, create a new relation to represent the relationship.
- The primary key of the new relation is a combination of the primary keys of the participating entities that hold the N (many) side.
- In most cases of an n-ary relationship, all the participating entities hold a **many** side.

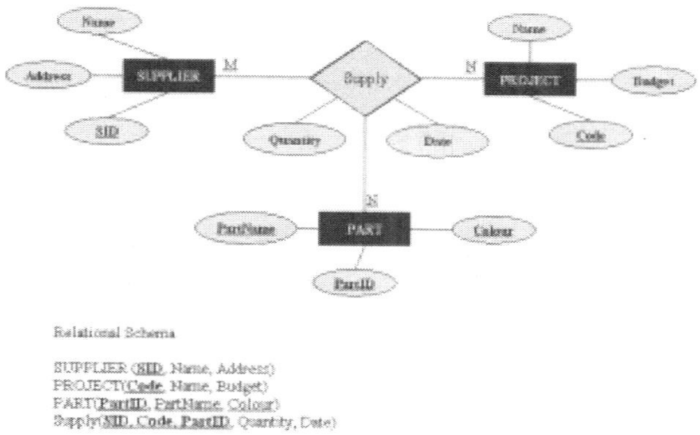


*Figure 8.10. Example of a ternary relationship.*

*Key Terms*

**alternate key**: all candidate keys not chosen as the primary key**candidate key**: a simple or composite key that is unique (no two rows in a table may have the same value) and minimal (every column is necessary)
**characteristic entities**: entities that provide more information about another table

**composite attributes**: attributes that consist of a hierarchy of attributes

**composite key**: composed of two or more attributes, but it must be minimal

**dependent entities**: these entities depend on other tables for their meaning

**derived attributes**: attributes that contain values calculated from other attributes

**derived entities**: see *dependent entities*

**EID**: employee identification (ID)

**entity**: a thing or object in the real world with an independent existence that can be differentiated from other objects

**entity relationship (ER) data model**: also called an ER schema, are represented by ER diagrams. These are well suited to data modelling for use with databases.

**entity relationship schema**: see *entity relationship data model*

**entity set**:a collection of entities of an entity type at a point of time

**entity type**: a collection of similar entities

**foreign key (FK)**: an attribute in a table that references the primary key in another table OR it can be null

**independent entity**: as the building blocks of a database, these entities are what other tables are based on

**kernel**: see *independent entity*

**key**: an attribute or group of attributes whose values can be used to uniquely identify an individual entity in an entity set

**multivalued attributes**: attributes that have a set of values for each entity

**n-ary**: multiple tables in a relationship

**null**: a special symbol, independent of data type, which means either unknown or inapplicable; it does not mean zero or blank

**recursive relationship**: see *unary relationship*

**relationships**: the associations or interactions between entities; used to connect related information between tables

**relationship strength**: based on how the primary key of a related entity is defined

**secondary key** an attribute used strictly for retrieval purposes

**simple attributes**: drawn from the atomic value domains

**SIN**: social insurance number

**single-valued attributes**: see *simple attributes*

**stored attribute**: saved physically to the database

**ternary relationship**: a relationship type that involves many to many relationships between three tables.

**unary relationship**: one in which a relationship exists between occurrences of the same entity set.

*Exercises*

1. What two concepts are ER modelling based on?
2. The database in Figure 8.11 is composed of two tables. Use this figure to answer questions 2.1 to 2.5.

**DIRECTOR**

| DIRNUM | DIRNAME | DIRDOB |
|---|---|---|
| 100 | J.Broadway | 01/08/39 |
| 101 | J.Namath | 11/12/48 |
| 102 | W.Blake | 06/15/44 |

**PLAY**

| PLAYNO | PLAYNAME | DIRNUM |
|---|---|---|
| 1001 | Cat on a cold bare roof | 102 |
| 1002 | Hold the mayo, pass the bread | 101 |
| 1003 | I never promised you coffee | 102 |
| 1004 | Silly putty goes to Texas | 100 |
| 1005 | See no sound, hear no sight | 101 |
| 1006 | Starstruck in Biloxi | 102 |
| 1007 | Stranger in parrot ice | 101 |

*Figure 8.11. Director and Play tables for question 2, by A. Watt.*

1. Identify the primary key for each table.
2. Identify the foreign key in the PLAY table.
3. Identify the candidate keys in both tables.
4. Draw the ER model.
5. Does the PLAY table exhibit referential integrity? Why or why not?

3. Define the following terms (you may need to use the Internet for some of these):
   schema
   host language
   data sublanguage
   data definition language
   unary relation
   foreign key
   virtual relation
   connectivity
   composite key
   linking table
4. The RRE Trucking Company database includes the three tables in Figure 8.12. Use Figure 8.12 to answer questions 4.1 to 4.5.

TRUCK

| TNUM | BASENUM | TYPENUM | TMILES | TBOUGHT | TSERIAL |
|---|---|---|---|---|---|
| 1001 | 501 | 1 | 5900.2 | 11/08/90 | aa-125 |
| 1002 | 502 | 2 | 64523.9 | 11/08/90 | ac-213 |
| 1003 | 501 | 2 | 32116.0 | 09/29/91 | ac-215 |
| 1004 | | 2 | 3256.9 | 01/14/92 | ac-315 |

BASE

| BASENUM | BASECITY | BASESTATE | BASEPHON | BASEMGR |
|---|---|---|---|---|
| 501 | Dallas | TX | 893-9870 | J. Jones |
| 502 | New York | NY | 234-7689 | K. Lee |

TYPE

| TYPENUM | TYPEDESC |
|---|---|
| 1 | single box, double axle |
| 2 | tandem trailer, single axle |

*Figure 8.12. Truck, Base and Type tables for question 4, by A. Watt.*

1. Identify the primary and foreign key(s) for each table.
2. Does the TRUCK table exhibit entity and referential integrity? Why or why not? Explain your answer.
3. What kind of relationship exists between the TRUCK and BASE tables?
4. How many entities does the TRUCK table contain ?
5. Identify the TRUCK table candidate key(s).

Customer

| CustID | CustName | AccntNo. |
|---|---|---|
| 100 | Joe Smith | 010839 |
| 101 | Andy Blake | 111248 |
| 102 | Sue Brown | 061544 |

BookOrders

| OrderID | Title | CustID | Price |
|---|---|---|---|
| 1001 | The Dark Tower | 102 | 12.00 |
| 1002 | Incubus Dreams | 101 | 19.99 |
| 1003 | Song of Susannah | 102 | 23.00 |
| 1004 | The Time Traveler's Wife | 100 | 21.00 |
| 1005 | The Dark Tower | 101 | 12.00 |
| 1006 | Tanequil | 102 | 15.00 |
| 1007 | Song of Susannah | 101 | 23.00 |

*Figure 8.13. Customer and BookOrders tables for question 5, by A. Watt.*

5. Suppose you are using the database in Figure 8.13, composed of the two tables. Use Figure 8.13 to answer questions 5.1 to 5.6.

    1. Identify the primary key in each table.

2. Identify the foreign key in the BookOrders table.
3. Are there any candidate keys in either table?
4. Draw the ER model.
5. Does the BookOrders table exhibit referential integrity? Why or why not?
6. Do the tables contain redundant data? If so which table(s) and what is the redundant data?

6. Looking at the student table in Figure 8.14, list all the possible candidate keys. Why did you select these?

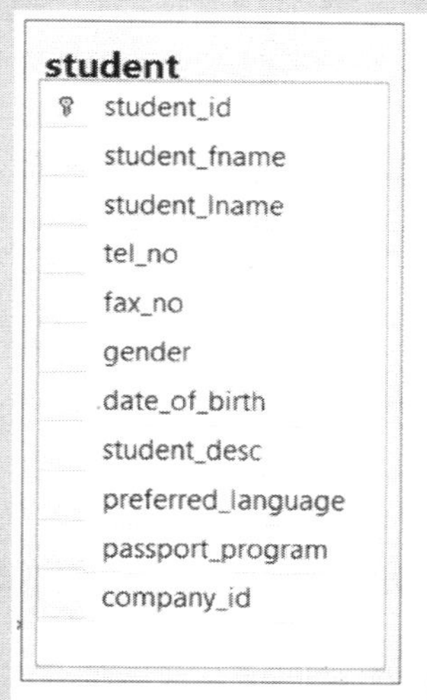


*Figure 8.14. Student table for question 6, by A. Watt.*

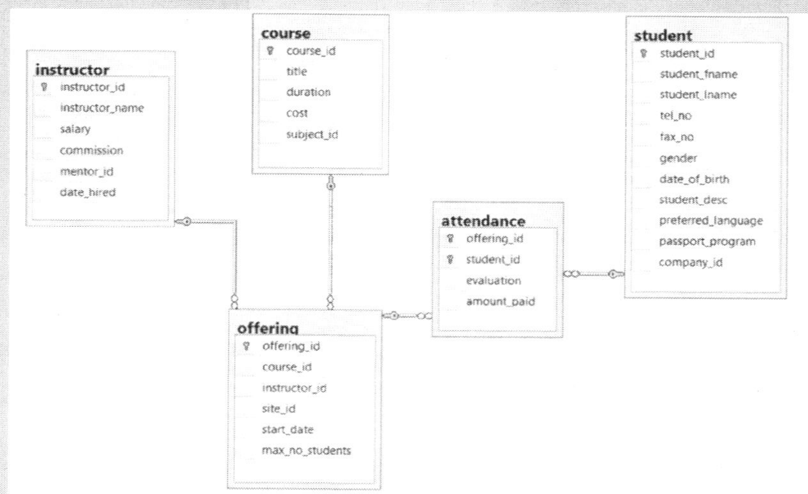


*Figure 8.15. ERD of school database for questions 7-10, by A. Watt.*

Use the ERD of a school database in Figure 8.15 to answer questions 7 to 10.

7. Identity all the kernels and dependent and characteristic entities in the ERD.

8. Which of the tables contribute to weak relationships? Strong relationships?
9. Looking at each of the tables in the school database in Figure 8.15, which attribute could have a NULL value? Why?
10. Which of the tables were created as a result of many to many relationships?

**Also see** *Appendix B: Sample ERD Exercises*

## Attribution



The following material was written by Adrienne Watt:

1. Nulls section and example
2. Key Terms
3. Exercises

# Chapter 9 Integrity Rules and Constraints

Constraints are a very important feature in a relational model. In fact, the relational model supports the well-defined theory of constraints on attributes or tables. Constraints are useful because they allow a designer to specify the semantics of data in the database. *Constraints* are the rules that force DBMSs to check that data satisfies the semantics.

## Domain Integrity

Domain restricts the values of attributes in the relation and is a constraint of the relational model. However, there are real-world semantics for data that cannot be specified if used only with domain constraints. We need more specific ways to state what data values are or are not allowed and which format is suitable for an attribute. For example, the Employee ID (EID) must be unique or the employee Birthdate is in the range [Jan 1, 1950, Jan 1, 2000]. Such information is provided in logical statements called *integrity constraints*.

There are several kinds of integrity constraints, described below.

### Entity integrity

To ensure *entity integrity*, it is required that every table have a primary key. Neither the PK nor any part of it can contain null values. This is because null values for the primary key mean we cannot identify some rows. For example, in the EMPLOYEE table, Phone cannot be a primary key since some people may not have a telephone.

### Referential integrity

*Referential integrity* requires that a foreign key must have a matching primary key or it must be null. This constraint is specified between two tables (parent and child); it maintains the correspondence between rows in these tables. It means the reference from a row in one table to another table must be valid.

Examples of referential integrity constraint in the Customer/Order database of the Company:

- Customer(**CustID**, CustName)
- Order(**OrderID**, CustID, OrderDate)

To ensure that there are no orphan records, we need to enforce referential integrity. An *orphan record* is one whose foreign key FK value is not found in the corresponding entity – the entity where the PK is located. Recall that a typical join is between a PK and FK.

The referential integrity constraint states that the customer ID (CustID) in the Order table must match a valid CustID in the Customer table. Most relational databases have declarative referential integrity. In other words, when the tables are created the referential integrity constraints are set up.

Here is another example from a Course/Class database:

- Course(**CrsCode**, DeptCode, Description)
- Class(**CrsCode, Section**, ClassTime)

The referential integrity constraint states that CrsCode in the Class table must match a valid CrsCode in the Course table. In this situation, it's not enough that the CrsCode and Section in the Class table make up the PK, we must also enforce referential integrity.

When setting up referential integrity it is important that the PK and FK have the same data types and come from the same domain, otherwise the relational database management system (RDBMS) will not allow the join. RDBMS is a popular database system that is based on the relational model introduced by E. F. Codd of IBM's San Jose Research Laboratory. Relational database systems are easier to use and understand than other database systems.

## Referential integrity in Microsoft Access

In Microsoft (MS) Access, referential integrity is set up by joining the PK in the Customer table to the CustID in the Order table. See Figure 9.1 for a view of how this is done on the Edit Relationships screen in MS Access.

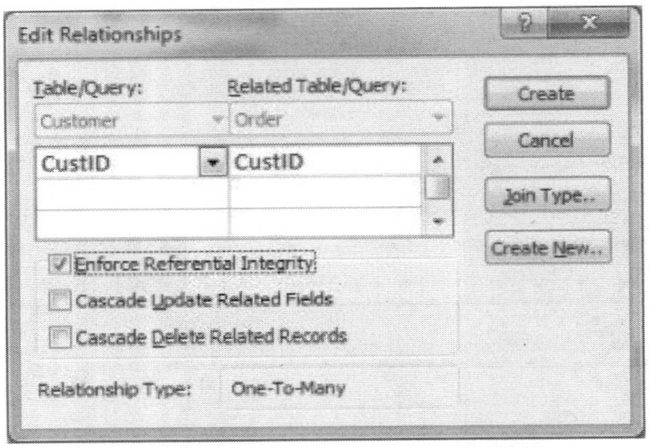


*Figure 9.1. Referential access in MS Access, by A. Watt.*

## Referential integrity using Transact-SQL (MS SQL Server)

When using Transact-SQL, the referential integrity is set when creating the Order table with the FK. Listed below are the statements showing the FK in the Order table referencing the PK in the Customer table.

```
CREATE TABLE Customer
( CustID INTEGER PRIMARY KEY,
CustName CHAR(35) )
```

```
CREATE TABLE Orders
( OrderID INTEGER PRIMARY KEY,
CustID INTEGER REFERENCES Customer(CustID),
OrderDate DATETIME )
```

### Foreign key rules

Additional foreign key rules may be added when setting referential integrity, such as what to do with the child rows (in the Orders table) when the record with the PK, part of the parent (Customer), is deleted or changed (updated). For example, the Edit Relationships window in MS Access (see Figure 9.1) shows two additional options for FK rules: Cascade Update and Cascade Delete. If these are not selected, the system will prevent the deletion or update of PK values in the parent table (Customer table) if a child record exists. The child record is any record with a matching PK.

In some databases, an additional option exists when selecting the Delete option called Set to Null. In this is chosen, the PK row is deleted, but the FK in the child table is set to NULL. Though this creates an orphan row, it is acceptable.

## Enterprise Constraints

Enterprise constraints – sometimes referred to as semantic constraints – are additional rules specified by users or database administrators and can be based on multiple tables.

Here are some examples.

- A class can have a maximum of 30 students.
- A teacher can teach a maximum of four classes per semester.
- An employee cannot take part in more than five projects.
- The salary of an employee cannot exceed the salary of the employee's manager.

## Business Rules

*Business rules* are obtained from users when gathering requirements. The requirements-gathering process is very important, and its results should be verified by the user before the database design is built. If the business rules are incorrect, the design will be incorrect, and ultimately the application built will not function as expected by the users.

Some examples of business rules are:

- A teacher can teach many students.
- A class can have a maximum of 35 students.
- A course can be taught many times, but by only one instructor.
- Not all teachers teach classes.

## Cardinality and connectivity

Business rules are used to determine cardinality and connectivity. *Cardinality* describes the relationship between two data tables by expressing the minimum and maximum number of entity occurrences associated with one occurrence of a related entity. In Figure 9.2, you can see that cardinality is represented by the innermost markings on the relationship symbol. In this figure, the cardinality is 0 (zero) on the right and 1 (one) on the left.

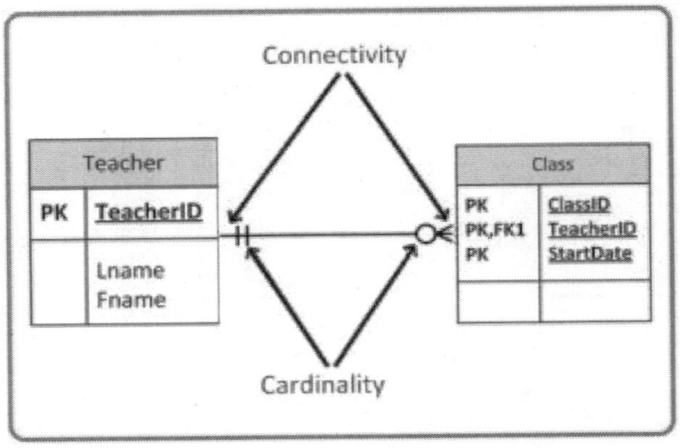


*Figure 9.2. Position of connectivity and cardinality on a relationship symbol, by A. Watt.*

The outermost symbol of the relationship symbol, on the other hand, represents the connectivity between the two tables. *Connectivity* is the relationship between two tables, e.g., one to one or one to many. The only time it is zero is when the FK can be null. When it comes to participation, there are three options to the relationship between these entities: either 0 (zero), 1 (one) or many. In Figure 9.2, for example, the connectivity is 1 (one) on the outer, left-hand side of this line and many on the outer, right-hand side.

Figure 9.3. shows the symbol that represents a one to many relationship.

*Figure 9.3.*

In Figure 9.4, both inner (representing cardinality) and outer (representing connectivity) markers are shown. The left side of this symbol is read as minimum 1 and maximum 1. On the right side, it is read as: minimum 1 and maximum many.

*Figure 9.4.*

## Relationship Types

The line that connects two tables, in an ERD, indicates the *relationship type* between the tables: either identifying or non-identifying. An *identifying relationship* will have a solid line (where the PK contains the FK). A *non-identifying relationship* is indicated by a broken line and does not contain the FK in the PK. See the section in Chapter 8 that discusses weak and strong relationships for more explanation.

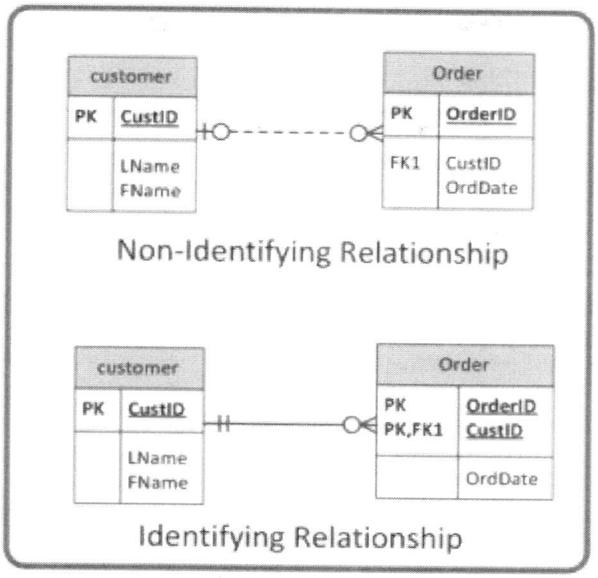


*Figure 9.5. Identifying and non-identifying relationship, by A. Watt.*

## Optional relationships

In an *optional relationship*, the FK can be null or the parent table does not need to have a corresponding child table occurrence. The symbol, shown in Figure 9.6, illustrates one type with a zero and three prongs (indicating many) which is interpreted as zero OR many.

*Figure 9.6.*

For example, if you look at the Order table on the right-hand side of Figure 9.7, you'll notice that a customer doesn't need to place an order to be a customer. In other words, the **many side** is optional.

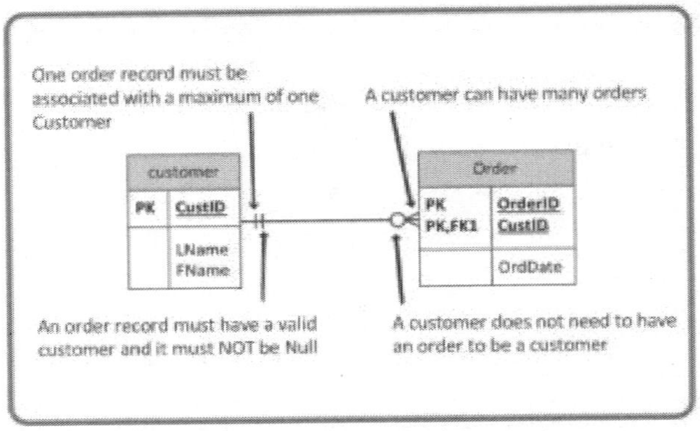


*Figure 9.7. Example usage of a zero to many optional relationship symbol, by A. Watt.*

The relationship symbol in Figure 9.7 can also be read as follows:

- Left side: The order entity must contain a minimum of one related entity in the Customer table and a maximum of one related entity.
- Right side: A customer can place a minimum of zero orders or a maximum of many orders.

Figure 9.8 shows another type of optional relationship symbol with a zero and one, meaning zero OR one. The **one side** is optional.

*Figure 9.8.*

Figure 9.9 gives an example of how a zero to one symbol might be used.

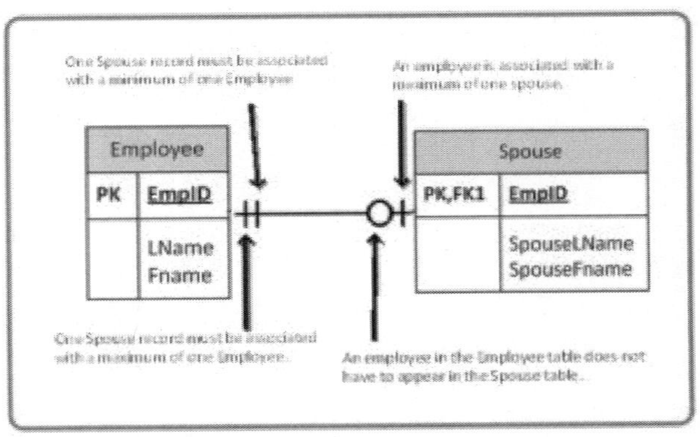


*Figure 9.9. Example usage of a zero to one optional relationship symbol, by A. Watt.*

## Mandatory relationships

In a *mandatory relationship*, one entity occurrence requires a corresponding entity occurrence. The symbol for this relationship shows *one and only one* as shown in Figure 9.10. The one side is mandatory.

*Figure 9.10*

See Figure 9.11 for an example of how the one and only one mandatory symbol is used.

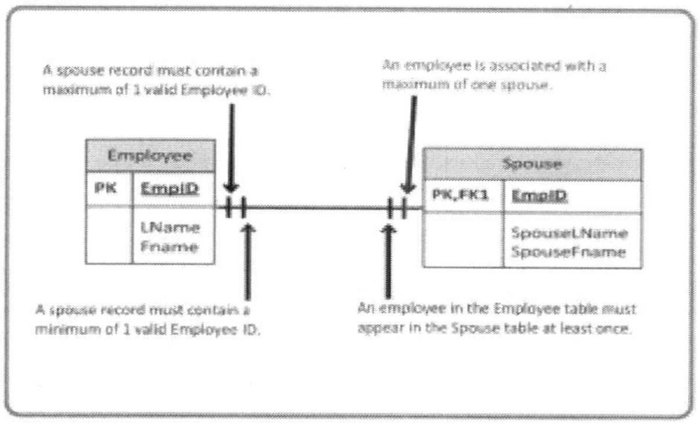


*Figure 9.11. Example of a one and only one mandatory relationship symbol, by A. Watt.*

Figure 9.12 illustrates what a one to many relationship symbol looks like where the **many side** is mandatory.

*Figure 9.12.*

Refer to Figure 9.13 for an example of how the one to many symbol may be used.

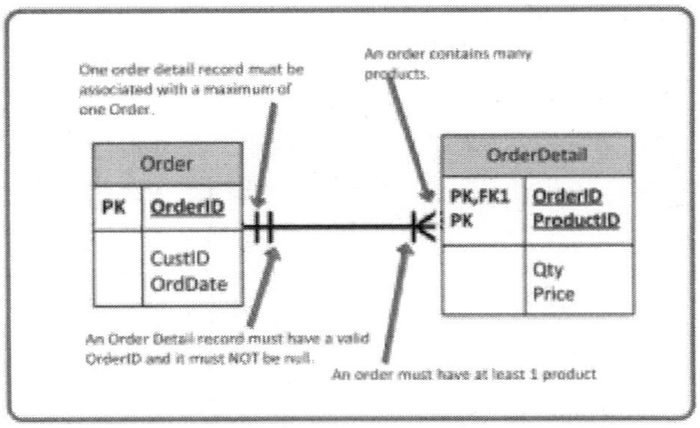


*Figure 9.13. Example of a one to many mandatory relationship symbol, by A. Watt.*

So far we have seen that the innermost side of a relationship symbol (on the left-side of the symbol in Figure 9.14) can have a 0 (zero) cardinality and a connectivity of many (shown on the right-side of the symbol in Figure 9.14), or one (not shown).

*Figure 9.14*

However, it cannot have a connectivity of 0 (zero), as displayed in Figure 9.15. The connectivity can only be 1.

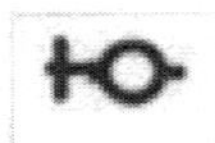

*Figure 9.15.*

The connectivity symbols show maximums. So if you think about it logically, if the connectivity symbol on the left side shows 0 (zero), then there would be no connection between the tables.

The way to read a relationship symbol, such as the one in Figure 9.16, is as follows.

- The CustID in the Order table must also be found in the Customer table a minimum of 0 and a maximum of 1 times.
- The 0 means that the CustID in the Order table may be null.
- The left-most 1 (right before the 0 representing connectivity) says that if there is a CustID in the Order table, it can only be in the Customer table once.
- When you see the 0 symbol for cardinality, you can assume two things: T

  1. the FK in the Order table allows nulls, and
  2. the FK is not part of the PK since PKs must not contain null values.

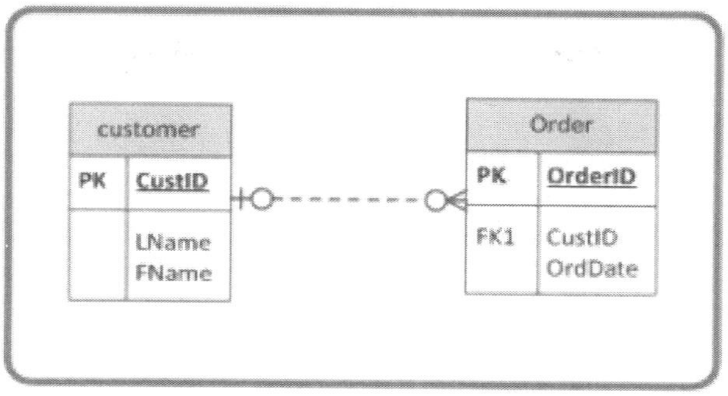


*Figure 9.16. The relationship between a Customer table and an Order table, by A. Watt.*

*Key Terms*

**business rules**: obtained from users when gathering requirements and are used to determine cardinality
**cardinality**: expresses the minimum and maximum number of entity occurrences associated with one occurrence of a related entity

**connectivity**: the relationship between two tables, e.g., one to one or one to many

**constraints**: the rules that force DBMSs to check that data satisfies the semantics

**entity integrity**: requires that every table have a primary key; neither the primary key, nor any part of it, can contain null values

**identifying relationship**: where the primary key contains the foreign key; indicated in an ERD by a solid line

**integrity constraints**: logical statements that state what data values are or are not allowed and which format is suitable for an attribute

**mandatory relationship**:one entity occurrence requires a corresponding entity occurrence.

**non-identifying relationship**: does not contain the foreign key in the primary key; indicated in an ERD by a dotted line

**optional relationship**: the FK can be null or the parent table does not need to have a corresponding child table occurrence

**orphan record**: a record whose foreign key value is not found in the corresponding entity – the entity where the primary key is located

**referential integrity**: requires that a foreign key must have a matching primary key or it must be null

**relational database management system (RDBMS)**: a popular database system based on the relational model introduced by E. F. Codd of IBM's San Jose Research Laboratory

**relationship type**: the type of relationship between two tables in an ERD (either identifying or non-identifying); this relationship is indicated by a line drawn between the two tables.

Exercises

*Read the following description and then answer questions 1-5 at the end.*

The swim club database in Figure 9.17 has been designed to hold information about students who are enrolled in swim classes. The following information is stored: students, enrollment, swim classes, pools where classes are held, instructors for the classes, and various levels of swim classes. Use Figure 9.17 to answer questions 1 to 5.

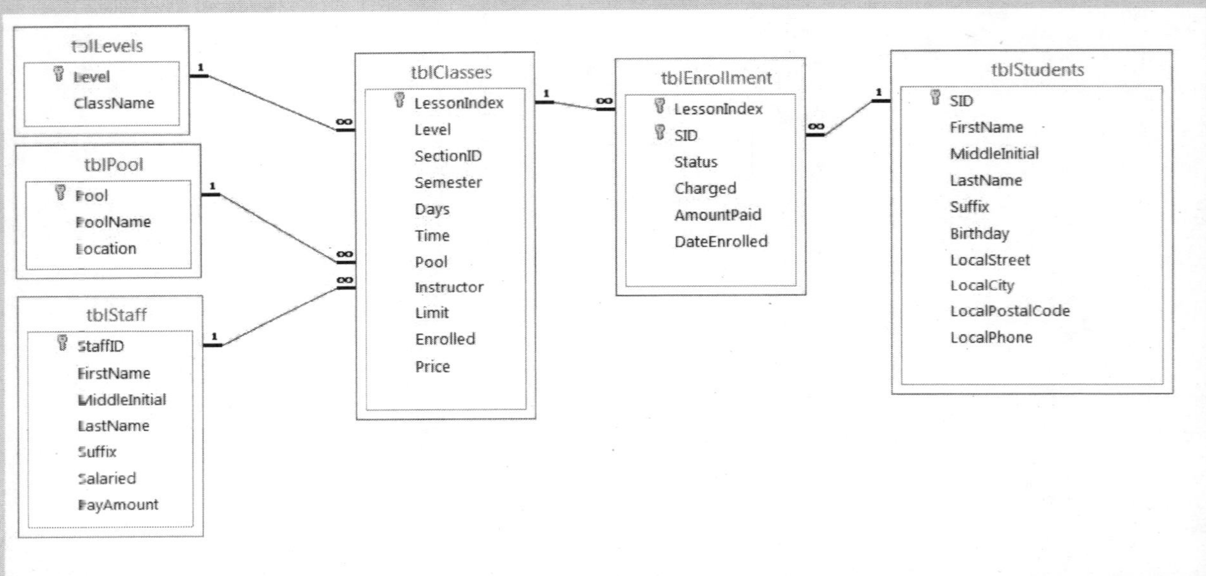


*Figure 9.17. ERD for questions 1-5. (Diagram by A. Watt.)*

The primary keys are identified below. The following data types are defined in the SQL Server.

**tblLevels**
Level – Identity PK
ClassName – text 20 – nulls are not allowed

**tblPool**
Pool – Identity PK

PoolName – text 20 – nulls are not allowed
Location – text 30

**tblStaff**
StaffID – Identity PK
FirstName – text 20
MiddleInitial – text 3
LastName – text 30
Suffix – text 3
Salaried – Bit
PayAmount – money

**tblClasses**
LessonIndex – Identity PK
Level – Integer FK
SectionID – Integer
Semester – TinyInt
Days – text 20
Time – datetime (formatted for time)
Pool – Integer FK
Instructor – Integer FK
Limit – TinyInt
Enrolled – TinyInt
Price – money

**tblEnrollment**
LessonIndex – Integer FK
SID – Integer FK (LessonIndex and SID) Primary Key
Status – text 30
Charged – bit
AmountPaid – money
DateEnrolled – datetime

**tblStudents**
SID – Identity PK
FirstName – text 20
MiddleInitial – text 3
LastName – text 30
Suffix – text 3
Birthday – datetime
LocalStreet – text 30
LocalCity – text 20
LocalPostalCode – text 6
LocalPhone – text 10

Implement this schema in SQL Server or access (you will need to pick comparable data types). Submit a screenshot of your ERD in the database.

1. Explain the relationship rules for each relationship (e.g., tblEnrollment and tblStudents: A student can enroll in many classes).
2. Identify cardinality for each relationship, assuming the following rules:

- A pool may or may not ever have a class.
- The levels table must always be associated with at least one class.
- The staff table may not have ever taught a class.
- All students must be enrolled in at least one class.
- The class must have students enrolled in it.
- The class must have a valid pool.
- The class may not have an instructor assigned.
- The class must always be associated with an existing level.

3. Which tables are weak and which tables are strong (covered in an earlier chapter)?
4. Which of the tables are non-identifying and which are identifying?

## Image Attributions

Figures 9.3, 9.4, 9.6, 9.8, 9.10, 9.12, 9.14 and 9.15 by A. Watt.

# Chapter 10 ER Modelling

One important theory developed for the entity relational (ER) model involves the notion of functional dependency (FD). The aim of studying this is to improve your understanding of relationships among data and to gain enough formalism to assist with practical database design.

Like constraints, FDs are drawn from the semantics of the application domain. Essentially, *functional dependencies* describe how individual attributes are related. FDs are a kind of constraint among attributes within a relation and contribute to a good relational schema design. In this chapter, we will look at:

- The basic theory and definition of functional dependency
- The methodology for improving schema designs, also called normalization

## Relational Design and Redundancy

Generally, a good relational database design must capture all of the necessary attributes and associations. The design should do this with a minimal amount of stored information and no redundant data.

In database design, redundancy is generally undesirable because it causes problems maintaining consistency after updates. However, redundancy can sometimes lead to performance improvements; for example, when redundancy can be used in place of a *join* to connect data. A *join* is used when you need to obtain information based on two related tables.

Consider Figure 10.1: customer 1313131 is displayed twice, once for account no. A-101 and again for account A-102. In this case, the customer number is not redundant, although there are deletion anomalies with the table. Having a separate customer table would solve this problem. However, if a branch address were to change, it would have to be updated in multiple places. If the customer number was left in the table as is, then you wouldn't need a branch table and no join would be required, and performance is improved .

| accountNo | balance | customer | branch | address | assets |
|---|---|---|---|---|---|
| A-101 | 500 | 1313131 | Downtown | Brooklyn | 9000000 |
| A-102 | 400 | 1313131 | Perryridge | Horseneck | 1700000 |
| A-113 | 600 | 9876543 | Round Hill | Horseneck | 8000000 |
| A-201 | 900 | 9876543 | Brighton | Brooklyn | 7100000 |
| A-215 | 700 | 1111111 | Mianus | Horseneck | 400000 |
| A-222 | 700 | 1111111 | Redwood | Palo Alto | 2100000 |
| A-305 | 350 | 1234567 | Round Hill | Horseneck | 8000000 |

Bank Accounts

*Figure 10.1. An example of redundancy used with bank accounts and branches.*

## Insertion Anomaly

An *insertion anomaly* occurs when you are inserting inconsistent information into a table. When we insert a new record, such as account no. A-306 in Figure 10.2, we need to check that the branch data is consistent with existing rows.

| accountNo | balance | customer | branch | address | assets |
|---|---|---|---|---|---|
| A-101 | 500 | 1313131 | Downtown | Brooklyn | 9000000 |
| A-102 | 400 | 1313131 | Perryridge | Horseneck | 1700000 |
| A-113 | 600 | 9876543 | Round Hill | Horseneck | 8000000 |
| A-201 | 900 | 9876543 | Brighton | Brooklyn | 7100000 |
| A-215 | 700 | 1111111 | Mianus | Horseneck | 400000 |
| A-222 | 700 | 1111111 | Redwood | Palo Alto | 2100000 |
| A-305 | 350 | 1234567 | Round Hill | Horseneck | 8000000 |
| A-306 | 800 | 1111111 | Round Hill | Horseneck | 8000800 |

Insertion anomaly - Insert account A-306 at Round Hill

*Figure 10.2. Example of an insertion anomaly.*

## Update Anomaly

If a branch changes address, such as the Round Hill branch in Figure 10.3, we need to update all rows referring to that branch. Changing existing information incorrectly is called an *update anomaly*.

| accountNo | balance | customer | branch | address | assets |
|---|---|---|---|---|---|
| A-101 | 500 | 1313131 | Downtown | Brooklyn | 9000000 |
| A-102 | 400 | 1313131 | Perryridge | Horseneck | 1700000 |
| A-113 | 600 | 9876543 | Round Hill | Palo Alto | 8000000 |
| A-201 | 900 | 9876543 | Brighton | Brooklyn | 7100000 |
| A-215 | 700 | 1111111 | Mianus | Horseneck | 400000 |
| A-222 | 700 | 1111111 | Redwood | Palo Alto | 2100000 |
| A-305 | 350 | 1234567 | Round Hill | Horseneck | 8000000 |

Update Anomaly - Round Hill branch address

*Figure 10.3. Example of an update anomaly.*

## Deletion Anomaly

A *deletion anomaly* occurs when you delete a record that may contain attributes that shouldn't be deleted. For instance, if we remove information about the last account at a branch, such as account A-101 at the Downtown branch in Figure 10.4, all of the branch information disappears.

| accountNo | balance | customer | branch | address | assets |
|---|---|---|---|---|---|
| A-101 | 500 | 1313131 | Downtown | Brooklyn | 9000000 |
| A-102 | 400 | 1313131 | Perryridge | Horseneck | 1700000 |
| A-113 | 600 | 9876543 | Round Hill | Horseneck | 8000000 |
| A-201 | 900 | 9876543 | Brighton | Brooklyn | 7100000 |
| A-215 | 700 | 1111111 | Mianus | Horseneck | 400000 |
| A-222 | 700 | 1111111 | Redwood | Palo Alto | 2100000 |
| A-305 | 350 | 1234567 | Round Hill | Horseneck | 8000000 |

Deletion anomaly - Bank Account

*Figure 10.4. Example of a deletion anomaly.*

The problem with deleting the A-101 row is we don't know where the Downtown branch is located and we lose all information regarding customer 1313131. To avoid these kinds of update or deletion problems, we need to decompose the original table into several smaller tables where each table has minimal overlap with other tables.

Each bank account table must contain information about one entity only, such as the Branch or Customer, as displayed in Figure 10.5.

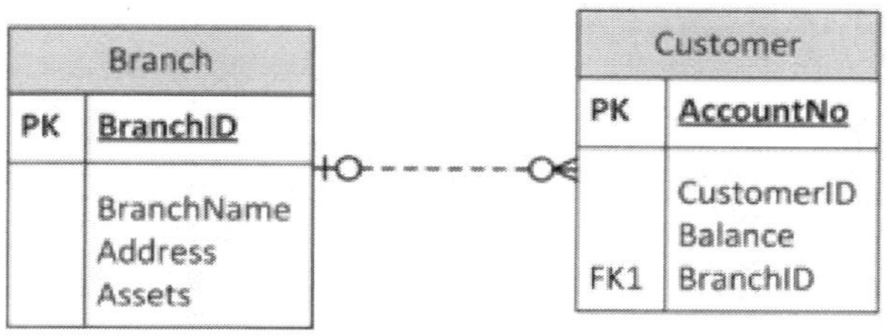


*Figure 10.5. Examples of bank account tables that contain one entity each, by A. Watt.*

Following this practice will ensure that when branch information is added or updated it will only affect one record. So, when customer information is added or deleted, the branch information will not be accidentally modified or incorrectly recorded.

## Example: employee project table and anomalies

Figure 10.6 shows an example of an employee project table. From this table, we can assume that:

1. EmpID and ProjectID are a composite PK.
2. Project ID determines Budget (i.e., Project P1 has a budget of 32 hours).

| EmpID | Budget | ProjectID | Hours |
|---|---|---|---|
| S75 | 32 | P1 | 7 |
| S75 | 40 | P2 | 3 |
| S79 | 32 | P1 | 4 |
| S79 | 27 | P3 | 1 |
| S80 | 40 | P2 | 5 |
| | 17 | P4 | |

*Figure 10.6. Example of an employee project table, by A. Watt.*

Next, let's look at some possible anomalies that might occur with this table during the following steps.

1. Action: Add row {S85,35,P1,9}
2. Problem: There are two tuples with conflicting budgets
3. Action: Delete tuple {S79, 27, P3, 1}
4. Problem: Step #3 deletes the budget for project P3
5. Action: Update tuple {S75, 32, P1, 7} to {S75, 35, P1, 7}
6. Problem: Step #5 creates two tuples with different values for project P1's budget
7. Solution: Create a separate table, each, for Projects and Employees, as shown in Figure 10.7.

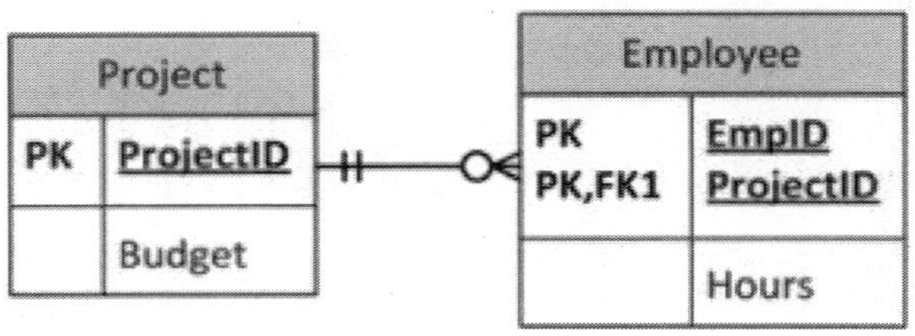


*Figure 10.7. Solution: separate tables for Project and Employee, by A. Watt.*

## How to Avoid Anomalies

The best approach to creating tables without anomalies is to ensure that the tables are normalized, and that's accomplished by understanding functional dependencies. FD ensures that all attributes in a table belong to that table. In other words, it will eliminate redundancies and anomalies.

## Example: separate Project and Employee tables

Project table

| ProjectID | Budget |
|---|---|
| P1 | 32 |
| P2 | 40 |
| P3 | 27 |
| P4 | 17 |

Employee table

| EmpID | ProjectID | Hours |
|---|---|---|
| S75 | P1 | 7 |
| S75 | P2 | 3 |
| S79 | P1 | 4 |
| S79 | P3 | 1 |
| S80 | P2 | 5 |

*Figure 10.8. Separate Project and Employee tables with data, by A. Watt.*

By keeping data separate using individual Project and Employee tables:

1. No anomalies will be created if a budget is changed.
2. No dummy values are needed for projects that have no employees assigned.
3. If an employee's contribution is deleted, no important data is lost.
4. No anomalies are created if an employee's contribution is added.

*Key Terms*

**deletion anomaly**: occurs when you delete a record that may contain attributes that shouldn't be deleted

**functional dependency (FD)**: describes how individual attributes are related

**insertion anomaly**: occurs when you are inserting inconsistent information into a table

**join**: used when you need to obtain information based on two related tables

**update anomaly**: changing existing information incorrectly

*Exercises*

1. Normalize Figure 10.9.

| Attribute Name | Sample Value | Sample Value | Sample Value |
|---|---|---|---|
| StudentID | 1 | 2 | 3 |
| StudentName | John Smith | Sandy Law | Sue Rogers |
| CourseID | 2 | 2 | 3 |
| CourseName | Programming Level 1 | Programming Level 1 | Business |
| Grade | 75% | 61% | 81% |
| CourseDate | Jan 5th, 2014 | Jan 5th, 2014 | Jan 7th, 2014 |

*Figure 10.9. Table for question 1, by A. Watt.*

2. Create a logical ERD for an online movie rental service (no many to many relationships). Use the following description of operations on which your business rules must be based:The online movie rental service classifies movie titles according to their type: comedy, western, classical, science fiction, cartoon, action, musical, and new release. Each type contains many possible titles, and most titles within a type are available in multiple copies. For example, note the following summary:TYPE TITLE
   Musical My Fair Lady (Copy 1)
   My Fair Lady (Copy 2)
   Oklahoma (Copy 1)
   Oklahoma (Copy 2)
   Oklahoma (Copy 3)
   etc.
3. What three data anomalies are likely to be the result of data redundancy? How can such anomalies be eliminated?

**Also see** *Appendix B: Sample ERD Exercises*

## Attribution

This chapter of *Database Design* (including images, except as otherwise noted) is a derivative copy of Relational Design Theory by Nguyen Kim Anh licensed under Creative Commons Attribution License 3.0 license

The following material was written by Adrienne Watt:

1. Example employee project table and anomalies
2. How to Avoid Anomalies
3. Key Terms
4. Exercises

# Chapter 11 Functional Dependencies

A *functional dependency* (FD) is a relationship between two attributes, typically between the PK and other non-key attributes within a table. For any relation R, attribute Y is functionally dependent on attribute X (usually the PK), if for every valid instance of X, that value of X uniquely determines the value of Y. This relationship is indicated by the representation below :

**X ––––> Y**

The left side of the above FD diagram is called the *determinant*, and the right side is the *dependent*. Here are a few examples.

In the first example, below, SIN determines Name, Address and Birthdate. Given SIN, we can determine any of the other attributes within the table.

**SIN ––––> Name, Address, Birthdate**

For the second example, SIN and Course determine the date completed (DateCompleted). This must also work for a composite PK.

**SIN, Course –––> DateCompleted**

The third example indicates that ISBN determines Title.

**ISBN ––––> Title**

## Rules of Functional Dependencies

Consider the following table of data r(R) of the relation schema R(ABCDE) shown in Table 11.1.

| A | B | C | D | E |
|---|---|---|---|---|
| a1 | b1 | c1 | d1 | e1 |
| a2 | b1 | C2 | d2 | e1 |
| a3 | b2 | C1 | d1 | e1 |
| a4 | b2 | C2 | d2 | e1 |
| a5 | b3 | C3 | d1 | e1 |

Table R

*Table 11.1. Functional dependency example, by A. Watt.*

As you look at this table, ask yourself: *What kind of dependencies can we observe among the attributes in Table R?* Since the values of A are unique (a1, a2, a3, etc.), it follows from the FD definition that:

A → B,   A → C,   A → D,   A → E

- It also follows that A →BC (or any other subset of ABCDE).
- This can be summarized as A →BCDE.
- From our understanding of primary keys, A is a primary key.

Since the values of E are always the same (all e1), it follows that:

A → E,  B → E,  C → E,  D → E

However, we cannot generally summarize the above with ABCD → E because, in general, A → E, B → E, AB → E.

Other observations:

1. Combinations of BC are unique, therefore BC → ADE.
2. Combinations of BD are unique, therefore BD → ACE.
3. If C values match, so do D values.
    1. Therefore, C → D
    2. However, D values don't determine C values
    3. So C does not determine D, and D does not determine C.

Looking at actual data can help clarify which attributes are dependent and which are determinants.

## Inference Rules

*Armstrong's axioms* are a set of inference rules used to infer all the functional dependencies on a relational database.

They were developed by William W. Armstrong. The following describes what will be used, in terms of notation, to explain these axioms.

Let R(U) be a relation scheme over the set of attributes U. We will use the letters X, Y, Z to represent any subset of and, for short, the union of two sets of attributes, instead of the usual X U Y.

## Axiom of reflexivity

This axiom says, if Y is a subset of X, then X determines Y (see Figure 11.1).

$$\text{If } Y \subseteq X \text{, then } X \rightarrow Y$$

*Figure 11.1. Equation for axiom of reflexivity.*

For example, **PartNo —> NT123** where X (PartNo) is composed of more than one piece of information; i.e., Y (NT) and partID (123).

## Axiom of augmentation

The axiom of augmentation, also known as a partial dependency, says if X determines Y, then XZ determines YZ for any Z (see Figure 11.2 ).

$$\text{If } X \rightarrow Y \text{, then } XZ \rightarrow YZ \text{ for any } Z$$

*Figure 11.2. Equation for axiom of augmentation.*

The axiom of augmentation says that every non-key attribute must be fully dependent on the PK. In the example shown below, StudentName, Address, City, Prov, and PC (postal code) are only dependent on the StudentNo, not on the StudentNo and Grade.

StudentNo, Course —> StudentName, Address, City, Prov, PC, Grade, DateCompleted

This situation is not desirable because every non-key attribute has to be fully dependent on the PK. In this situation, student information is only partially dependent on the PK (StudentNo).

To fix this problem, we need to break the original table down into two as follows:

- Table 1: StudentNo, Course, Grade, DateCompleted
- Table 2: StudentNo, StudentName, Address, City, Prov, PC

## Axiom of transitivity

The axiom of transitivity says if X determines Y, and Y determines Z, then X must also determine Z (see Figure 11.3).

$$\text{If } X \rightarrow Y \text{ and } Y \rightarrow Z\text{, then } X \rightarrow Z$$

*Figure 11.3. Equation for axiom of transitivity.*

The table below has information not directly related to the student; for instance, ProgramID and ProgramName should have a table of its own. ProgramName is not dependent on StudentNo; it's dependent on ProgramID.

StudentNo —> StudentName, Address, City, Prov, PC, ProgramID, ProgramName

This situation is not desirable because a non-key attribute (ProgramName) depends on another non-key attribute (ProgramID).

To fix this problem, we need to break this table into two: one to hold information about the student and the other to hold information about the program.

- Table 1: StudentNo —> StudentName, Address, City, Prov, PC, ProgramID
- Table 2: ProgramID —> ProgramName

However we still need to leave an FK in the student table so that we can identify which program the student is enrolled in.

## Union

This rule suggests that if two tables are separate, and the PK is the same, you may want to consider putting them together. It states that if X determines Y and X determines Z then X must also determine Y and Z (see Figure 11.4).

$$\text{If } X \rightarrow Y \text{ and } X \rightarrow Z \text{ then } X \rightarrow YZ$$

*Figure 11.4. Equation for the Union rule.*

For example, if:

- SIN —> EmpName
- SIN —> SpouseName

You may want to join these two tables into one as follows:

SIN -> EmpName, SpouseName

Some database administrators (DBA) might choose to keep these tables separated for a couple of reasons. One, each table describes a different entity so the entities should be kept apart. Two, if SpouseName is to be left NULL most of the time, there is no need to include it in the same table as EmpName.

## Decomposition

Decomposition is the reverse of the Union rule. If you have a table that appears to contain two entities that are determined by the same PK, consider breaking them up into two tables. This rule states that if X determines Y and Z, then X determines Y and X determines Z separately (see Figure 11.5).

$$\text{If } X \rightarrow YZ \text{ then } X \rightarrow Y \text{ and } X \rightarrow Z$$

*Figure 11.5. Equation for decompensation rule.*

## Dependency Diagram

A dependency diagram, shown in Figure 11.6, illustrates the various dependencies that might exist in a *non-normalized table.* A non-normalized table is one that has data redundancy in it.

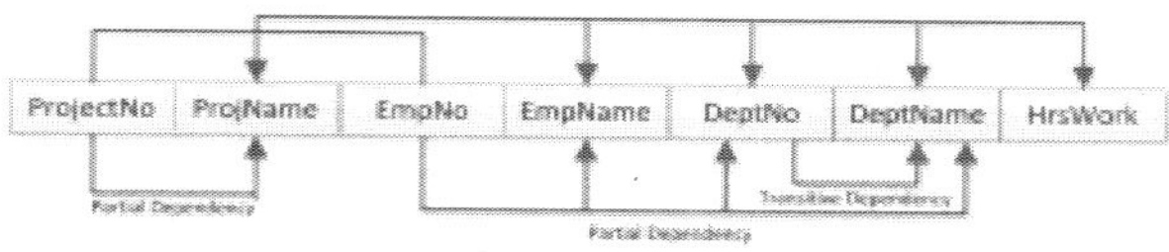


*Figure 11.6. Dependency diagram.*

The following dependencies are identified in this table:

- ProjectNo and EmpNo, combined, are the PK.
- Partial Dependencies:
    - ProjectNo —> ProjName
    - EmpNo —> EmpName, DeptNo,
    - ProjectNo, EmpNo —> HrsWork
- Transitive Dependency:
    - DeptNo —> DeptName

*Key Terms*

**Armstrong's axioms**: a set of inference rules used to infer all the functional dependencies on a relational database**DBA**: database administrator
**decomposition**: a rule that suggests if you have a table that appears to contain two entities that are determined by the same PK, consider breaking them up into two tables

**dependent**: the right side of the functional dependency diagram

**determinant**: the left side of the functional dependency diagram

**functional dependency (FD):** a relationship between two attributes, typically between the PK and other non-key attributes within a table

**non-normalized table**: a table that has data redundancy in it

**Union**: a rule that suggests that if two tables are separate, and the PK is the same, consider putting them together

*Exercises*

See Chapter 12.

## Attributions

This chapter of *Database Design* (including images, except as otherwise noted) is a derivative copy of Armstrong's axioms by Wikipedia the Free Encyclopedia licensed under Creative Commons Attribution-ShareAlike 3.0 Unported

The following material was written by Adrienne Watt:

1. some of Rules of Functional Dependencies
2. Key Terms

# Chapter 12 Normalization

Normalization should be part of the database design process. However, it is difficult to separate the normalization process from the ER modelling process so the two techniques should be used concurrently.

Use an entity relation diagram (ERD) to provide the big picture, or macro view, of an organization's data requirements and operations. This is created through an iterative process that involves identifying relevant entities, their attributes and their relationships.

Normalization procedure focuses on characteristics of specific entities and represents the micro view of entities within the ERD.

## What Is Normalization?

*Normalization* is the branch of relational theory that provides design insights. It is the process of determining how much redundancy exists in a table. The goals of normalization are to:

- Be able to characterize the level of redundancy in a relational schema
- Provide mechanisms for transforming schemas in order to remove redundancy

Normalization theory draws heavily on the theory of functional dependencies. Normalization theory defines six normal forms (NF). Each normal form involves a set of dependency properties that a schema must satisfy and each normal form gives guarantees about the presence and/or absence of update anomalies. This means that higher normal forms have less redundancy, and as a result, fewer update problems.

## Normal Forms

All the tables in any database can be in one of the normal forms we will discuss next. Ideally we only want minimal redundancy for PK to FK. Everything else should be derived from other tables. There are six normal forms, but we will only look at the first four, which are:

- First normal form (1NF)
- Second normal form (2NF)
- Third normal form (3NF)
- Boyce-Codd normal form (BCNF)

BCNF is rarely used.

## First Normal Form (1NF)

In the *first normal form*, only single values are permitted at the intersection of each row and column; hence, there are no repeating groups.

To normalize a relation that contains a repeating group, remove the repeating group and form two new relations.

The PK of the new relation is a combination of the PK of the original relation plus an attribute from the newly created relation for unique identification.

### Process for 1NF

We will use the **Student_Grade_Report** table below, from a School database, as our example to explain the process for 1NF.

> **Student_Grade_Report** (StudentNo, StudentName, Major, CourseNo, CourseName, InstructorNo, InstructorName, InstructorLocation, Grade)

- In the Student Grade Report table, the repeating group is the course information. A student can take many courses.
- Remove the repeating group. In this case, it's the course information for each student.
- Identify the PK for your new table.
- The PK must uniquely identify the attribute value (StudentNo and CourseNo).
- After removing all the attributes related to the course and student, you are left with the student course table (**StudentCourse**).
- The Student table (**Student**) is now in first normal form with the repeating group removed.
- The two new tables are shown below.

> **Student** (StudentNo, StudentName, Major)

> **StudentCourse** (StudentNo, CourseNo, CourseName, InstructorNo, InstructorName, InstructorLocation, Grade)

## How to update 1NF anomalies

**StudentCourse** (StudentNo, CourseNo, CourseName, InstructorNo, InstructorName, InstructorLocation, Grade)

- To add a new course, we need a student.
- When course information needs to be updated, we may have inconsistencies.
- To delete a *student*, we might also delete critical information about a course.

# Second Normal Form (2NF)

For the *second normal form*, the relation must first be in 1NF. The relation is automatically in 2NF if, and only if, the PK comprises a single attribute.

If the relation has a composite PK, then each non-key attribute must be fully dependent on the entire PK and not on a subset of the PK (i.e., there must be no partial dependency or augmentation).

## Process for 2NF

To move to 2NF, a table must first be in 1NF.

- The Student table is already in 2NF because it has a single-column PK.
- When examining the Student Course table, we see that not all the attributes are fully dependent on the PK; specifically, all course information. The only attribute that is fully dependent is grade.
- Identify the new table that contains the course information.
- Identify the PK for the new table.
- The three new tables are shown below.

**Student** (StudentNo, StudentName, Major)

**CourseGrade** (StudentNo, CourseNo, Grade)

**CourseInstructor** (CourseNo, CourseName, InstructorNo, InstructorName, InstructorLocation)

### How to update 2NF anomalies

- When adding a new instructor, we need a course.
- Updating course information could lead to inconsistencies for instructor information.
- Deleting a course may also delete instructor information.

## Third Normal Form (3NF)

To be in *third normal form*, the relation must be in second normal form. Also all transitive dependencies must be removed; a non-key attribute may not be functionally dependent on another non-key attribute.

### Process for 3NF

- Eliminate all dependent attributes in transitive relationship(s) from each of the tables that have a transitive relationship.
- Create new table(s) with removed dependency.
- Check new table(s) as well as table(s) modified to make sure that each table has a determinant and that no table contains inappropriate dependencies.
- See the four new tables below.

**Student** (StudentNo, StudentName, Major)

**CourseGrade** (StudentNo, CourseNo, Grade)

**Course** (CourseNo, CourseName, InstructorNo)

**Instructor** (InstructorNo, InstructorName, InstructorLocation)

At this stage, there should be no anomalies in third normal form. Let's look at the dependency diagram (Figure 12.1) for this example. The first step is to remove repeating groups, as discussed above.

**Student** (StudentNo, StudentName, Major)

**StudentCourse** (StudentNo, CourseNo, CourseName, InstructorNo, InstructorName, InstructorLocation, Grade)

To recap the normalization process for the School database, review the dependencies shown in Figure 12.1.

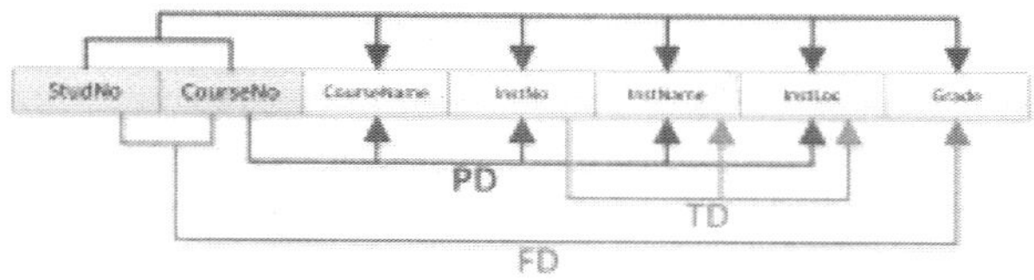


*Figure 12.1 Dependency diagram, by A. Watt.*

The abbreviations used in Figure 12.1 are as follows:

- PD: partial dependency
- TD: transitive dependency
- FD: full dependency (Note: FD typically stands for **functional** dependency. Using FD as an abbreviation for full dependency is only used in Figure 12.1.)

## Boyce-Codd Normal Form (BCNF)

When a table has more than one candidate key, anomalies may result even though the relation is in 3NF. *Boyce-Codd normal form* is a special case of 3NF. A relation is in BCNF if, and only if, every determinant is a candidate key.

### BCNF Example 1

Consider the following table (**St_Maj_Adv**).

| **Student_id** | **Major** | **Advisor** |
|---|---|---|
| 111 | Physics | Smith |
| 111 | Music | Chan |
| 320 | Math | Dobbs |
| 671 | Physics | White |
| 803 | Physics | Smith |

The *semantic rules* (business rules applied to the database) for this table are:

1. Each Student may major in several subjects.
2. For each Major, a given Student has only one Advisor.
3. Each Major has several Advisors.
4. Each Advisor advises only one Major.
5. Each Advisor advises several Students in one Major.

The functional dependencies for this table are listed below. The first one is a candidate key; the second is not.

1. Student_id, Major ––> Advisor
2. Advisor ––> Major

Anomalies for this table include:

1. Delete – student deletes advisor info
2. Insert – a new advisor needs a student
3. Update – inconsistencies

**Note**: No single attribute is a candidate key.

PK can be Student_id, Major or Student_id, Advisor.

To reduce the **St_Maj_Adv** relation to BCNF, you create two new tables:

1. **St_Adv** (Student_id, Advisor)
2. **Adv_Maj** (Advisor, Major)

**St_Adv** table

| **Student_id** | **Advisor** |
|---|---|
| 111 | Smith |
| 111 | Chan |
| 320 | Dobbs |
| 671 | White |
| 803 | Smith |

**Adv_Maj** table

| **Advisor** | **Major** |
|---|---|
| Smith | Physics |
| Chan | Music |
| Dobbs | Math |
| White | Physics |

## BCNF Example 2

Consider the following table (**Client_Interview**).

| ClientNo | InterviewDate | InterviewTime | StaffNo | RoomNo |
|---|---|---|---|---|
| CR76 | 13-May-02 | 10.30 | SG5 | G101 |
| CR56 | 13-May-02 | 12.00 | SG5 | G101 |
| CR74 | 13-May-02 | 12.00 | SG37 | G102 |
| CR56 | 1-July-02 | 10.30 | SG5 | G102 |

FD1 – ClientNo, InterviewDate –> InterviewTime, StaffNo, RoomNo (PK)

FD2 – staffNo, interviewDate, interviewTime –> clientNO (candidate key: CK)

FD3 – roomNo, interviewDate, interviewTime –> staffNo, clientNo (CK)

FD4 – staffNo, interviewDate –> roomNo

A relation is in BCNF if, and only if, every determinant is a candidate key. We need to create a table that incorporates the first three FDs (**Client_Interview2** table) and another table (**StaffRoom** table) for the fourth FD.

**Client_Interview2** table

| ClientNo | InterviewDate | InterViewTime | StaffNo |
|---|---|---|---|
| CR76 | 13-May-02 | 10.30 | SG5 |
| CR56 | 13-May-02 | 12.00 | SG5 |
| CR74 | 13-May-02 | 12.00 | SG37 |
| CR56 | 1-July-02 | 10.30 | SG5 |

**StaffRoom** table

| StaffNo | InterviewDate | RoomNo |
|---|---|---|
| SG5 | 13-May-02 | G101 |
| SG37 | 13-May-02 | G102 |
| SG5 | 1-July-02 | G102 |

## Normalization and Database Design

During the normalization process of database design, make sure that proposed entities meet required normal form before table structures are created. Many real-world databases have been improperly designed or burdened with anomalies if improperly modified during the course of time. You may be asked to redesign and modify existing databases. This can be a large undertaking if the tables are not properly normalized.

*Key Terms and Abbrevations*

**Boyce-Codd normal form (BCNF):** a special case of 3rd NF

**first normal form (1NF)**: only single values are permitted at the intersection of each row and column so there are no repeating groups

**normalization**: the process of determining how much redundancy exists in a table

**second normal form (2NF)**: the relation must be in 1NF and the PK comprises a single attribute

**semantic rules**: business rules applied to the database

**third normal form (3NF)**: the relation must be in 2NF and all transitive dependencies must be removed; a non-key attribute may not be functionally dependent on another non-key attribute

*Exercises*

**Complete chapters 11 and 12 before doing these exercises.**

1. What is normalization?
2. When is a table in 1NF?
3. When is a table in 2NF?
4. When is a table in 3NF?
5. Identify and discuss each of the indicated dependencies in the dependency diagram shown in Figure 12.2.

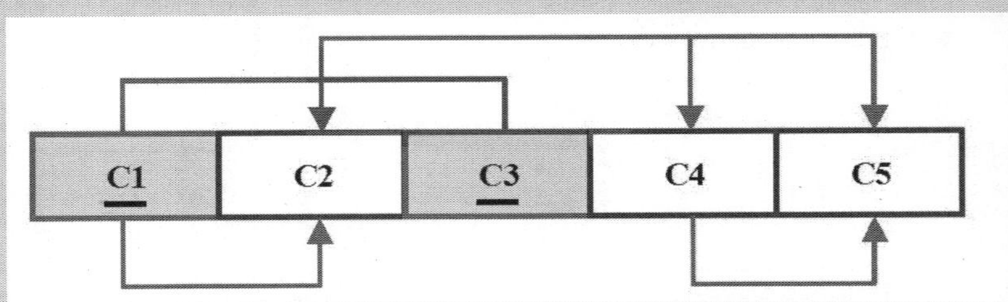


*Figure 12.2 For question 5, by A. Watt.*

6. To keep track of students and courses, a new college uses the table structure in Figure 12.3. Draw the dependency diagram for this table.

| Attribute Name | Sample Value | Sample Value | Sample Value |
|---|---|---|---|
| StudentID | 1 | 2 | 3 |
| StudentName | John Smith | Sandy Law | Sue Rogers |
| CourseID | 2 | 2 | 3 |
| CourseName | Programming Level 1 | Programming Level 1 | Business |
| Grade | 75% | 61% | 81% |
| CourseDate | Jan 5th, 2014 | Jan 5th, 2014 | Jan 7th, 2014 |

*Figure 12.3 For question 6, by A. Watt.*

7. Using the dependency diagram you just drew, show the tables (in their third normal form) you would create to fix the problems you encountered. Draw the dependency diagram for the fixed table.
8. An agency called Instant Cover supplies part-time/temporary staff to hotels in Scotland. Figure 12.4 lists the time spent by agency staff working at various hotels. The national insurance number (NIN) is unique for every member of staff. Use Figure 12.4 to answer questions (a) and (b).

| NIN | ContractNo | Hours | eName | hNo | hLoc |
|---|---|---|---|---|---|
| 1135 | C1024 | 16 | Smith J. | H25 | East Killbride |
| 1057 | C1024 | 24 | Hocine D. | H25 | East Killbride |
| 1068 | C1025 | 28 | White T. | H4 | Glasgow |
| 1135 | C1025 | 15 | Smith J. | H4 | Glasgow |

*Figure 12.4 For question 8, by A. Watt.*

   1. This table is susceptible to update anomalies. Provide examples of insertion, deletion and update anomalies.
   2. Normalize this table to third normal form. State any assumptions.

9. Fill in the blanks:

   1. ________________________ produces a lower normal form.
   2. Any attribute whose value determines other values within a row is called a(n) ________________________.
   3. An attribute that cannot be further divided is said to display ________________________.
   4. ________________________ refers to the level of detail represented by the values stored in a table's row.
   5. A relational table must not contain ________________________ groups.

**Also see** *Appendix B: Sample ERD Exercises*

## Bibliography

Nguyen Kim Anh, *Relational Design Theory*. OpenStax CNX. 8 Jul 2009 Retrieved July 2014 from http://cnx.org/contents/606cc532-0b1d-419d-a0ec-ac4e2e2d533b@1@1

Russell, Gordon. Chapter 4 – Normalisation. *Database eLearning*. N.d. Retrived July 2014 from db.grussell.org/ch4.html

# Chapter 13 Database Development Process

A core aspect of software engineering is the subdivision of the development process into a series of phases, or steps, each of which focuses on one aspect of the development. The collection of these steps is sometimes referred to as the *software development life cycle* (SDLC). The software product moves through this life cycle (sometimes repeatedly as it is refined or redeveloped) until it is finally retired from use. Ideally, each phase in the life cycle can be checked for correctness before moving on to the next phase.

## Software Development Life Cycle – Waterfall

Let us start with an overview of the *waterfall model* such as you will find in most software engineering textbooks. This waterfall figure, seen in Figure 13.1, illustrates a general waterfall model that could apply to any computer system development. It shows the process as a strict sequence of steps where the output of one step is the input to the next and all of one step has to be completed before moving onto the next.

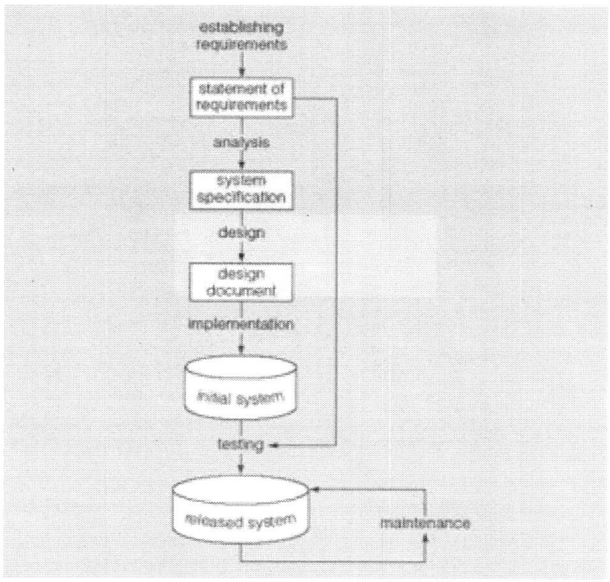


*Figure 13.1. Waterfall model.*

We can use the *waterfall process* as a means of identifying the tasks that are required, together with the input and output for each activity. What is important is the scope of the activities, which can be summarized as follows:

- *Establishing requirements* involves consultation with, and agreement among, stakeholders about what they want from a system, expressed as a statement of requirements.
- *Analysis* starts by considering the statement of requirements and finishes by producing a system specification. The specification is a formal representation of what a system should do, expressed in terms that are independent of how it may be realized.
- *Design* begins with a system specification, produces design documents and provides a detailed description of how

a system should be constructed.

- *Implementation* is the construction of a computer system according to a given design document and taking into account the environment in which the system will be operating (e.g., specific hardware or software available for the development). Implementation may be staged, usually with an initial system that can be validated and tested before a final system is released for use.
- *Testing* compares the implemented system against the design documents and requirements specification and produces an acceptance report or, more usually, a list of errors and bugs that require a review of the analysis, design and implementation processes to correct (testing is usually the task that leads to the waterfall model iterating through the life cycle).
- *Maintenance* involves dealing with changes in the requirements or the implementation environment, bug fixing or porting of the system to new environments (e.g., migrating a system from a standalone PC to a UNIX workstation or a networked environment). Since maintenance involves the analysis of the changes required, design of a solution, implementation and testing of that solution over the lifetime of a maintained software system, the waterfall life cycle will be repeatedly revisited.

## Database Life Cycle

We can use the waterfall cycle as the basis for a model of database development that incorporates three assumptions:

1. We can separate the development of a database – that is, specification and creation of a schema to define data in a database – from the user processes that make use of the database.
2. We can use the three-schema architecture as a basis for distinguishing the activities associated with a schema.
3. We can represent the constraints to enforce the semantics of the data once within a database, rather than within every user process that uses the data.

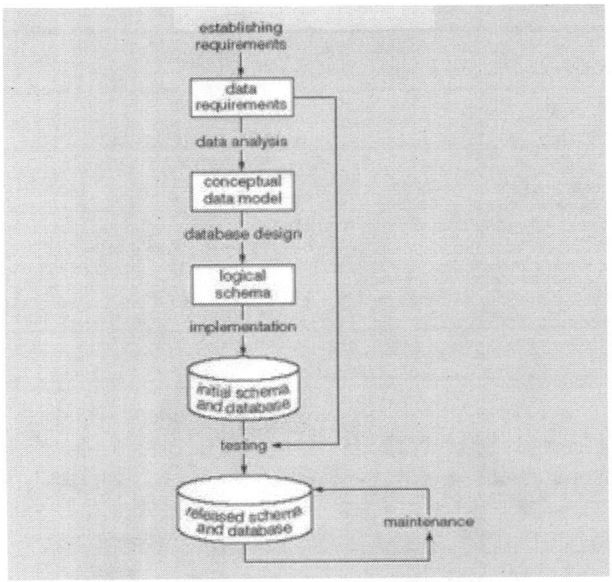


*Figure 13.2. A waterfall model of the activities and their outputs for database development.*

Using these assumptions and Figure 13.2, we can see that this diagram represents a model of the activities and their outputs for database development. It is applicable to any class of DBMS, not just a relational approach.

Database application development is the process of obtaining real-world requirements, analyzing requirements, designing the data and functions of the system, and then implementing the operations in the system.

## Requirements Gathering

The first step is *requirements gathering*. During this step, the database designers have to interview the customers (database users) to understand the proposed system and obtain and document the data and functional requirements. The result of this step is a document that includes the detailed requirements provided by the users.

Establishing requirements involves consultation with, and agreement among, all the users as to what persistent data they want to store along with an agreement as to the meaning and interpretation of the data elements. The data administrator plays a key role in this process as they overview the business, legal and ethical issues within the organization that impact on the data requirements.

The *data requirements document* is used to confirm the understanding of requirements with users. To make sure that it is easily understood, it should not be overly formal or highly encoded. The document should give a concise summary of all users' requirements – not just a collection of individuals' requirements – as the intention is to develop a single shared database.

The requirements should not describe how the data is to be processed, but rather what the data items are, what attributes they have, what constraints apply and the relationships that hold between the data items.

## Analysis

Data analysis begins with the statement of data requirements and then produces a conceptual data model. The aim of analysis is to obtain a detailed description of the data that will suit user requirements so that both high and low level properties of data and their use are dealt with. These include properties such as the possible range of values that can be permitted for attributes (e.g., in the school database example, the student course code, course title and credit points).

The conceptual data model provides a shared, formal representation of what is being communicated between clients and developers during database development – it is focused on the data in a database, irrespective of the eventual use of that data in user processes or implementation of the data in specific computer environments. Therefore, a conceptual data model is concerned with the meaning and structure of data, but not with the details affecting how they are implemented.

The conceptual data model then is a formal representation of what data a database should contain and the constraints the data must satisfy. This should be expressed in terms that are independent of how the model may be implemented. As a result, analysis focuses on the questions, "What is required?" not "How is it achieved?"

## Logical Design

Database design starts with a conceptual data model and produces a specification of a logical schema; this will determine the specific type of database system (network, relational, object-oriented) that is required. The relational representation is still independent of any specific DBMS; it is another conceptual data model.

We can use a relational representation of the conceptual data model as input to the logical design process. The output of this stage is a detailed relational specification, the logical schema, of all the tables and constraints needed to satisfy the description of the data in the conceptual data model. It is during this design activity that choices are made as to which tables are most appropriate for representing the data in a database. These choices must take into account various design criteria including, for example, flexibility for change, control of duplication and how best to represent the constraints. It is the tables defined by the logical schema that determine what data are stored and how they may be manipulated in the database.

Database designers familiar with relational databases and SQL might be tempted to go directly to implementation after they have produced a conceptual data model. However, such a direct transformation of the relational representation to SQL tables does not necessarily result in a database that has all the desirable properties: completeness, integrity, flexibility, efficiency and usability. A good conceptual data model is an essential first step towards a database with these properties, but that does not mean that the direct transformation to SQL tables automatically produces a good database. This first step will accurately represent the tables and constraints needed to satisfy the conceptual data model description, and so will satisfy the completeness and integrity requirements, but it may be inflexible or offer poor usability. The first design is then flexed to improve the quality of the database design. *Flexing* is a term that is intended to capture the simultaneous ideas of bending something for a different purpose and weakening aspects of it as it is bent.

Figure 13.3 summarizes the iterative (repeated) steps involved in database design, based on the overview given. Its main purpose is to distinguish the general issue of what tables should be used from the detailed definition of the constituent parts of each table – these tables are considered one at a time, although they are not independent of each other. Each iteration that involves a revision of the tables would lead to a new design; collectively they are usually referred to as *second-cut designs*, even if the process iterates for more than a single loop.

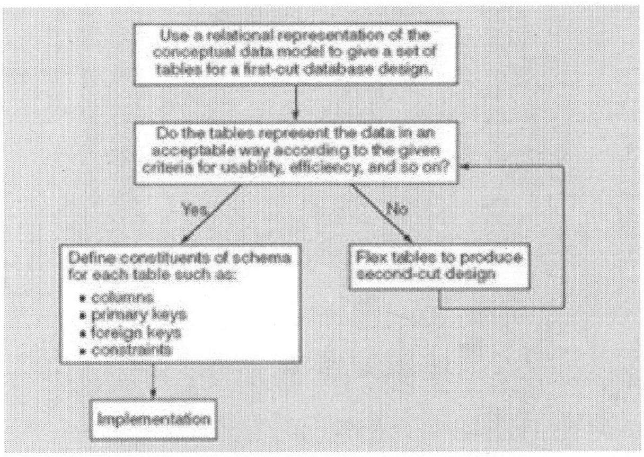


*Figure 13.3. A summary of the iterative steps involved in database design.*

First, for a given conceptual data model, it is not necessary that all the user requirements it represents be satisfied by a single database. There can be various reasons for the development of more than one database, such as the need for independent operation in different locations or departmental control over "their" data. However, if the collection of databases contains duplicated data and users need to access data in more than one database, then there are possible reasons that one database can satisfy multiple requirements, or issues related to data replication and distribution need to be examined.

Second, one of the assumptions about database development is that we can separate the development of a database from the development of user processes that make use of it. This is based on the expectation that, once a database has been implemented, all data required by currently identified user processes have been defined and can be accessed; but we also require flexibility to allow us to meet future requirements changes. In developing a database for some applications, it may be possible to predict the common requests that will be presented to the database and so we can optimize our design for the most common requests.

Third, at a detailed level, many aspects of database design and implementation depend on the particular DBMS being used. If the choice of DBMS is fixed or made prior to the design task, that choice can be used to determine design criteria rather than waiting until implementation. That is, it is possible to incorporate design decisions for a specific DBMS rather than produce a generic design and then tailor it to the DBMS during implementation.

It is not uncommon to find that a single design cannot simultaneously satisfy all the properties of a good database. So it is important that the designer has prioritized these properties (usually using information from the requirements specification); for example, to decide if integrity is more important than efficiency and whether usability is more important than flexibility in a given development.

At the end of our design stage, the logical schema will be specified by SQL data definition language (DDL) statements, which describe the database that needs to be implemented to meet the user requirements.

## Implementation

Implementation involves the construction of a database according to the specification of a logical schema. This will include the specification of an appropriate storage schema, security enforcement, external schema and so on. Implementation is heavily influenced by the choice of available DBMSs, database tools and operating environment. There are additional tasks beyond simply creating a database schema and implementing the constraints – data must be entered into the tables, issues relating to the users and user processes need to be addressed, and the management activities associated with wider aspects of corporate data management need to be supported. In keeping with the DBMS approach, we want as many of these concerns as possible to be addressed within the DBMS. We look at some of these concerns briefly now.

In practice, implementation of the logical schema in a given DBMS requires a very detailed knowledge of the specific features and facilities that the DBMS has to offer. In an ideal world, and in keeping with good software engineering practice, the first stage of implementation would involve matching the design requirements with the best available implementing tools and then using those tools for the implementation. In database terms, this might involve choosing vendor products with DBMS and SQL variants most suited to the database we need to implement. However, we don't live in an ideal world and more often than not, hardware choice and decisions regarding the DBMS will have been made well in advance of consideration of the database design. Consequently, implementation can involve additional flexing of the design to overcome any software or hardware limitations.

## Realizing the Design

After the logical design has been created, we need our database to be created according to the definitions we have produced. For an implementation with a relational DBMS, this will probably involve the use of SQL to create tables and constraints that satisfy the logical schema description and the choice of appropriate storage schema (if the DBMS permits that level of control).

One way to achieve this is to write the appropriate SQL DDL statements into a file that can be executed by a DBMS so that there is an independent record, a text file, of the SQL statements defining the database. Another method is to work interactively using a database tool like SQL Server Management Studio or Microsoft Access. Whatever mechanism is used to implement the logical schema, the result is that a database, with tables and constraints, is defined but will contain no data for the user processes.

## Populating the Database

After a database has been created, there are two ways of populating the tables – either from existing data or through the use of the user applications developed for the database.

For some tables, there may be existing data from another database or data files. For example, in establishing a database for a hospital, you would expect that there are already some records of all the staff that have to be included in the database. Data might also be brought in from an outside agency (address lists are frequently brought in from external companies) or produced during a large data entry task (converting hard-copy manual records into computer files can be done by a data entry agency). In such situations, the simplest approach to populate the database is to use the import and export facilities found in the DBMS.

Facilities to import and export data in various standard formats are usually available (these functions are also known in some systems as loading and unloading data). Importing enables a file of data to be copied directly into a table. When data are held in a file format that is not appropriate for using the import function, then it is necessary to prepare an application program that reads in the old data, transforms them as necessary and then inserts them into the database using SQL code specifically produced for that purpose. The transfer of large quantities of existing data into a database is referred to as a *bulk load*. Bulk loading of data may involve very large quantities of data being loaded, one table at a time so you may find that there are DBMS facilities to postpone constraint checking until the end of the bulk loading.

## Guidelines for Developing an ER Diagram

**Note:** These are general guidelines that will assist in developing a strong basis for the actual database design (the logical model).

1. Document all entities discovered during the information-gathering stage.
2. Document all attributes that belong to each entity. Select candidate and primary keys. Ensure that all non-key attributes for each entity are full-functionally dependent on the primary key.
3. Develop an initial ER diagram and review it with appropriate personnel. (Remember that this is an iterative process.)
4. Create new entities (tables) for multivalued attributes and repeating groups. Incorporate these new entities (tables) in the ER diagram. Review with appropriate personnel.

5. Verify ER modeling by normalizing tables.

*Key Terms*

**analysis**: starts by considering the statement of requirements and finishes by producing a system specification**bulk load**: the transfer of large quantities of existing data into a database
**data requirements document**:used to confirm the understanding of requirements with the user

**design**: begins with a system specification, produces design documents and provides a detailed description of how a system should be constructed

**establishing requirements**: involves consultation with, and agreement among, stakeholders as to what they want from a system; expressed as a statement of requirements

**flexing**: a term that captures the simultaneous ideas of bending something for a different purpose and weakening aspects of it as it is bent

**implementation**: the construction of a computer system according to a given design document

**maintenance**: involves dealing with changes in the requirements or the implementation environment, bug fixing or porting of the system to new environments

**requirements gathering**: a process during which the database designer interviews the database user to understand the proposed system and obtain and document the data and functional requirements

**second-cut designs**:the collection of iterations that each involves a revision of the tables that lead to a new design

**software development life cycle (SDLC)**: the series of steps involved in the database development process

**testing**: compares the implemented system against the design documents and requirements specification and produces an acceptance report

**waterfall model**: shows the database development process as a strict sequence of steps where the output of one step is the input to the next

**waterfall process**: a means of identifying the tasks required for database development, together with the input and output for each activity (see *waterfall model*)

*Exercises*

1. Describe the waterfall model. List the steps.
2. What does the acronym SDLC mean, and what does an SDLC portray?
3. What needs to be modified in the waterfall model to accommodate database design?
4. Provide the iterative steps involved in database design.

## Attribution



The following material was written by Adrienne Watt:

1. Key Terms
2. Exercises

# Chapter 14 Database Users

## End Users

End users are the people whose jobs require access to a database for querying, updating and generating reports.

### Application user

The application user is someone who accesses an existing application program to perform daily tasks.

### Sophisticated user

Sophisticated users are those who have their own way of accessing the database. This means they do not use the application program provided in the system. Instead, they might define their own application or describe their need directly by using query languages. These specialized users maintain their personal databases by using ready-made program packages that provide easy-to-use menu driven commands, such as MS Access.

### Application Programmers

These users implement specific application programs to access the stored data. They must be familiar with the DBMSs to accomplish their task.

### Database Administrators (DBA)

This may be one person or a group of people in an organization responsible for authorizing access to the database, monitoring its use and managing all of the resources to support the use of the entire database system.

*Key Terms*

**application programmer**: user who implements specific application programs to access the stored data
**application user**: accesses an existing application program to perform daily tasks.

**database administrator (DBA)**: responsible for authorizing access to the database, monitoring its use and managing all the resources to support the use of the entire database system

**end user**: people whose jobs require access to a database for querying, updating and generating reports

**sophisticated user**: those who use other methods, other than the application program, to access the database

There are no exercises provided for this chapter.

# Chapter 15 SQL Structured Query Language

*Structured Query Language* (SQL) is a database language designed for managing data held in a relational database management system. SQL was initially developed by IBM in the early 1970s (Date 1986). The initial version, called SEQUEL (Structured English Query Language), was designed to manipulate and retrieve data stored in IBM's quasi-relational database management system, System R. Then in the late 1970s, Relational Software Inc., which is now Oracle Corporation, introduced the first commercially available implementation of SQL, Oracle V2 for VAX computers.

Many of the currently available relational DBMSs, such as Oracle Database, Microsoft SQL Server (shown in Figure 15.1), MySQL, IBM DB2, IBM Informix and Microsoft Access, use SQL.

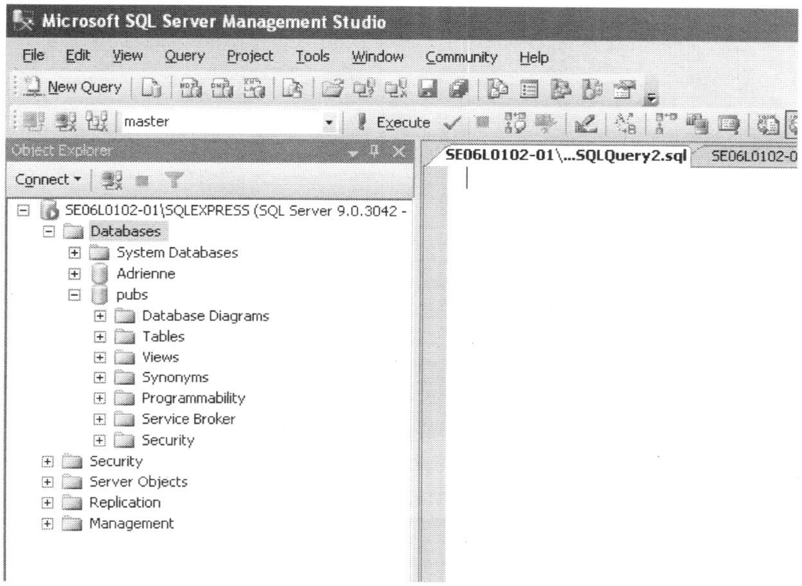


*Figure 15.1. Example of Microsoft SQL Server, by A. Watt.*

In a DBMS, the SQL database language is used to:

- Create the database and table structures
- Perform basic data management chores (add, delete and modify)
- Perform complex queries to transform raw data into useful information

In this chapter, we will focus on using SQL to create the database and table structures, mainly using SQL as a data definition language (*DDL*). In Chapter 16, we will use SQL as a data manipulation language (*DML*) to insert, delete, select and update data within the database tables.

## Create Database

The major SQL DDL statements are CREATE DATABASE and CREATE/DROP/ALTER TABLE. The SQL statement CREATE is used to create the database and table structures.

**Example: CREATE DATABASE SW**

A new database named **SW** is created by the SQL statement CREATE DATABASE SW. Once the database is created, the next step is to create the database tables.

The general format for the CREATE TABLE command is:

```
CREATE TABLE <tablename>
(
ColumnName, Datatype, Optional Column Constraint,
ColumnName, Datatype, Optional Column Constraint,
Optional table Constraints
);
```

Tablename is the name of the database table such as **Employee**. Each field in the CREATE TABLE has three parts (see above):

1. ColumnName
2. Data type
3. Optional Column Constraint

## ColumnName

The ColumnName must be unique within the table. Some examples of ColumnNames are FirstName and LastName.

## Data Type

The data type, as described below, must be a system data type or a user-defined data type. Many of the data types have a size such as CHAR(35) or Numeric(8,2).

**Bit** –Integer data with either a 1 or 0 value

**Int** –Integer (whole number) data from -2^31 (-2,147,483,648) through 2^31 – 1 (2,147,483,647)

**Smallint** –Integer data from 2^15 (-32,768) through 2^15 – 1 (32,767)

**Tinyint** –Integer data from 0 through 255

**Decimal** –Fixed precision and scale numeric data from -10^38 -1 through 10^38

**Numeric** –A synonym for **decimal**

**Timestamp** –A database-wide unique number

**Uniqueidentifier** –A globally unique identifier (GUID)

**Money** – Monetary data values from -2^63 (-922,337,203,685,477.5808) through 2^63 – 1 (+922,337,203,685,477.5807), with accuracy to one-ten-thousandth of a monetary unit

**Smallmoney** –Monetary data values from -214,748.3648 through +214,748.3647, with accuracy to one-ten-thousandth of a monetary unit

**Float** –Floating precision number data from -1.79E + 308 through 1.79E + 308

**Real** –Floating precision number data from -3.40E + 38 through 3.40E + 38

**Datetime** –Date and time data from January 1, 1753, to December 31, 9999, with an accuracy of one-three-hundredths of a second, or 3.33 milliseconds

**Smalldatetime** –Date and time data from January 1, 1900, through June 6, 2079, with an accuracy of one minute

**Char** –Fixed-length non-Unicode character data with a maximum length of 8,000 characters

**Varchar** –Variable-length non-Unicode data with a maximum of 8,000 characters

**Text** –Variable-length non-Unicode data with a maximum length of 2^31 – 1 (2,147,483,647) characters

**Binary** –Fixed-length binary data with a maximum length of 8,000 bytes

**Varbinary** –Variable-length binary data with a maximum length of 8,000 bytes

**Image** – Variable-length binary data with a maximum length of 2^31 – 1 (2,147,483,647) bytes

## Optional Column Constraints

The Optional ColumnConstraints are NULL, NOT NULL, UNIQUE, PRIMARY KEY and DEFAULT, used to initialize a value for a new record. The column constraint NULL indicates that null values are allowed, which means that a row can be created without a value for this column. The column constraint NOT NULL indicates that a value must be supplied when a new row is created.

To illustrate, we will use the SQL statement CREATE TABLE EMPLOYEES to create the employees table with 16 attributes or fields.

```
USE SW
CREATE TABLE EMPLOYEES
(
EmployeeNo          CHAR(10)      NOT NULL      UNIQUE,
DepartmentName      CHAR(30)      NOT NULL      DEFAULT "Human Resources",
FirstName           CHAR(25)      NOT NULL,
```

```
LastName            CHAR(25)     NOT NULL,
Category            CHAR(20)     NOT NULL,
HourlyRate          CURRENCY     NOT NULL,
TimeCard            LOGICAL      NOT NULL,
HourlySalaried      CHAR(1)      NOT NULL,
EmpType             CHAR(1)      NOT NULL,
Terminated          LOGICAL      NOT NULL,
ExemptCode          CHAR(2)      NOT NULL,
Supervisor          LOGICAL      NOT NULL,
SupervisorName      CHAR(50)     NOT NULL,
BirthDate           DATE         NOT NULL,
CollegeDegree       CHAR(5)      NOT NULL,
CONSTRAINT          Employee_PK  PRIMARY KEY(EmployeeNo
);
```

The first field is EmployeeNo with a field type of CHAR. For this field, the field length is 10 characters, and the user cannot leave this field empty (NOT NULL).

Similarly, the second field is DepartmentName with a field type CHAR of length 30. After all the table columns are defined, a table constraint, identified by the word CONSTRAINT, is used to create the primary key:

```
CONSTRAINT    EmployeePK    PRIMARY KEY(EmployeeNo)
```

We will discuss the constraint property further later in this chapter.

Likewise, we can create a Department table, a Project table and an Assignment table using the CREATE TABLE SQL DDL command as shown in the below example.

```
USE SW
CREATE TABLE DEPARTMENT
(
DepartmentName Char(35)  NOT NULL,
BudgetCode     Char(30)  NOT NULL,
OfficeNumber   Char(15)  NOT NULL,
Phone          Char(15)  NOT NULL,
CONSTRAINT DEPARTMENT_PK PRIMARY KEY(DepartmentName)
);
```

In this example, a project table is created with seven fields: ProjectID, ProjectName, Department, MaxHours, StartDate, and EndDate.

```
USE SW
CREATE TABLE PROJECT
(
ProjectID      Int  NOT NULL IDENTITY (1000,100),
ProjectName    Char(50) NOT NULL,
Department     Char(35) NOT NULL,
MaxHours       Numeric(8,2)  NOT NULL DEFAULT 100,
StartDate      DateTime NULL,
EndDate        DateTime NULL,
CONSTRAINT     ASSIGNMENT_PK  PRIMARY KEY(ProjectID)
);
```

In this last example, an assignment table is created with three fields: ProjectID, EmployeeNumber, and HoursWorked. The assignment table is used to record who (EmployeeNumber) and how much time(HoursWorked) an employee worked on the particular project(ProjectID).

```
USE SW
CREATE TABLE ASSIGNMENT
(
ProjectID      Int  NOT NULL,
EmployeeNumber Int  NOT NULL,
HoursWorked    Numeric(6,2)  NULL,
);
```

## Table Constraints

Table constraints are identified by the CONSTRAINT keyword and can be used to implement various constraints described below.

### IDENTITY constraint

We can use the optional column constraint IDENTITY to provide a unique, incremental value for that column. Identity columns are often used with the PRIMARY KEY constraints to serve as the unique row identifier for the table. The IDENTITY property can be assigned to a column with a tinyint, smallint, int, decimal or numeric data type. This constraint:

- Generates sequential numbers
- Does not enforce entity integrity

- Only one column can have the IDENTITY property
- Must be defined as an integer, numeric or decimal data type
- Cannot update a column with the IDENTITY property
- Cannot contain NULL values
- Cannot bind defaults and default constraints to the column

For IDENTITY[(seed, increment)]

- Seed – the initial value of the identity column
- Increment – the value to add to the last increment column

We will use another database example to further illustrate the SQL DDL statements by creating the table tblHotel in this HOTEL database.

```
CREATE TABLE  tblHotel
(
HotelNo          Int            IDENTITY (1,1),
Name             Char(50)       NOT NULL,
Address          Char(50)       NULL,
City             Char(25)       NULL,
)
```

UNIQUE constraint

The UNIQUE constraint prevents duplicate values from being entered into a column.

- Both PK and UNIQUE constraints are used to enforce entity integrity.
- Multiple UNIQUE constraints can be defined for a table.
- When a UNIQUE constraint is added to an existing table, the existing data is always validated.
- A UNIQUE constraint can be placed on columns that accept nulls. *Only one row can be NULL.*
- A UNIQUE constraint automatically creates a unique index on the selected column.

This is the general syntax for the UNIQUE constraint:

```
[CONSTRAINT constraint_name]
UNIQUE [CLUSTERED | NONCLUSTERED]
(col_name [, col_name2 [..., col_name16]])
[ON segment_name]
```

This is an examle using the UNIQUE constraint.

```
CREATE TABLE EMPLOYEES
(
EmployeeNo          CHAR(10)        NOT NULL        UNIQUE,
)
```

## FOREIGN KEY constraint

The FOREIGN KEY (FK) constraint defines a column, or combination of columns, whose values match the PRIMARY KEY (PK) of another table.

- Values in an FK are automatically updated when the PK values in the associated table are updated/changed.
- FK constraints must reference PK or the UNIQUE constraint of another table.
- The number of columns for FK must be same as PK or UNIQUE constraint.
- If the WITH NOCHECK option is used, the FK constraint will not validate existing data in a table.
- No index is created on the columns that participate in an FK constraint.

This is the general syntax for the FOREIGN KEY constraint:

```
[CONSTRAINT constraint_name]
[FOREIGN KEY (col_name [, col_name2 [..., col_name16]])]
REFERENCES [owner.]ref_table [(ref_col [, ref_col2 [..., ref_col16]])]
```

In this example, the field HotelNo in the tblRoom table is a FK to the field HotelNo in the tblHotel table shown previously.

```
USE HOTEL
GO
CREATE TABLE  tblRoom
(
HotelNo       Int             NOT NULL ,
RoomNo  Int           NOT NULL,
Type            Char(50)        NULL,
Price           Money           NULL,
PRIMARY KEY (HotelNo, RoomNo),
FOREIGN KEY (HotelNo) REFERENCES tblHotel
)
```

## CHECK constraint

The CHECK constraint restricts values that can be entered into a table.

- It can contain search conditions similar to a WHERE clause.
- It can reference columns in the same table.
- The data validation rule for a CHECK constraint must evaluate to a boolean expression.
- It can be defined for a column that has a rule bound to it.

This is the general syntax for the CHECK constraint:

```
[CONSTRAINT constraint_name]
CHECK [NOT FOR REPLICATION] (expression)
```

In this example, the Type field is restricted to have only the types 'Single', 'Double', 'Suite' or 'Executive'.

```
USE HOTEL
GO
CREATE TABLE  tblRoom
(
HotelNo        Int              NOT NULL,
RoomNo  Int              NOT NULL,
Type           Char(50)      NULL,
Price      Money                NULL,
PRIMARY KEY (HotelNo, RoomNo),
FOREIGN KEY (HotelNo) REFERENCES tblHotel
CONSTRAINT Valid_Type
CHECK (Type IN ('Single', 'Double', 'Suite', 'Executive'))
)
```

In this second example, the employee hire date should be before January 1, 2004, or have a salary limit of $300,000.

```
GO
CREATE TABLE SALESREPS
(
Empl_num    Int Not Null
CHECK (Empl_num BETWEEN 101 and 199),
Name           Char (15),
Age     Int       CHECK (Age >= 21),
```

```
Quota              Money              CHECK (Quota >= 0.0),
HireDate     DateTime,
CONSTRAINT  QuotaCap CHECK ((HireDate < "01-01-2004") OR (Quota <=300000))
)
```

## DEFAULT constraint

The DEFAULT constraint is used to supply a value that is automatically added for a column if the user does not supply one.

- A column can have only one DEFAULT.
- The DEFAULT constraint cannot be used on columns with a timestamp data type or identity property.
- DEFAULT constraints are automatically bound to a column when they are created.

The general syntax for the DEFAULT constraint is:

```
[CONSTRAINT constraint_name]
DEFAULT {constant_expression | niladic-function | NULL}
[FOR col_name]
```

This example sets the default for the city field to 'Vancouver'.

```
USE HOTEL
ALTER TABLE tblHotel
Add CONSTRAINT df_city DEFAULT 'Vancouver' FOR City
```

# User Defined Types

User defined types are always based on system-supplied data type. They can enforce data integrity and they allow nulls.

To create a user-defined data type in SQL Server, choose types under "Programmability" in your database. Next, right click and choose 'New' ->'User-defined data type' or execute the sp_addtype system stored procedure. After this, type:

```
sp_addtype ssn, 'varchar(11)', 'NOT NULL'
```

This will add a new user-defined data type called SIN with nine characters.

In this example, the field EmployeeSIN uses the user-defined data type SIN.

```
CREATE TABLE SINTable
(
EmployeeID      INT Primary Key,
EmployeeSIN   SIN,
CONSTRAINT CheckSIN
CHECK (EmployeeSIN LIKE
' [0-9][0-9][0-9] – [0-9][0-9] [0-9] – [0-9][0-9][0-9] ')
)
```

## ALTER TABLE

You can use ALTER TABLE statements to add and drop constraints.

- ALTER TABLE allows columns to be removed.
- When a constraint is added, all existing data are verified for violations.

In this example, we use the ALTER TABLE statement to the IDENTITY property to a ColumnName field.

```
USE HOTEL
GO
ALTER TABLE  tblHotel
ADD CONSTRAINT unqName UNIQUE (Name)
```

Use the ALTER TABLE statement to add a column with the IDENTITY property such as ALTER TABLE TableName.

```
ADD
ColumnName      int   IDENTITY(seed, increment)
```

## DROP TABLE

The DROP TABLE will remove a table from the database. Make sure you have the correct database selected.

```
DROP TABLE tblHotel
```

Executing the above SQL DROP TABLE statement will remove the table tblHotel from the database.

*Key Terms*

**DDL**: abbreviation for *data definition language*
**DML**: abbreviation for *data manipulation language*

**SEQUEL**: acronym for *Structured English Query Language*; designed to manipulate and retrieve data stored in IBM's quasi-relational database management system, System R

**Structured Query Language (SQL)**: a database language designed for managing data held in a relational database management system

*Exercises*

1. Using the information for the Chapter 9 exercise, implement the schema using Transact SQL (show SQL statements for each table). Implement the constraints as well.
2. Create the table shown here in SQL Server and show the statements you used.
   Table: Employee

| ATTRIBUTE (FIELD) NAME | DATA DECLARATION |
|---|---|
| EMP_NUM | CHAR(3) |
| EMP_LNAME | VARCHAR(15) |
| EMP_FNAME | VARCHAR(15) |
| EMP_INITIAL | CHAR(1) |
| EMP_HIREDATE | DATE |
| JOB_CODE | CHAR(3) |

3. Having created the table structure in question 2, write the SQL code to enter the rows for the table shown in Figure 15.1.

| EMP_NUM | EMP_LNAME | EMP_FNAME | EMP_INITIAL | EMP_HIREDATE | JOB_CODE |
|---|---|---|---|---|---|
| 101 | News | John | G | 08-Nov-00 | 502 |
| 102 | Senior | David | H | 12-Jul-89 | 501 |
| 103 | Arbough | June | E | 01-Dec-96 | 500 |
| 104 | Ramoras | Anne | K | 15-Nov-87 | 501 |
| 105 | Johnson | Alice | K | 01-Feb-93 | 502 |
| 106 | Smithfield | William | | 22-Jun-04 | 500 |
| 107 | Alonzo | Maria | D | 10-Oct-93 | 500 |
| 108 | Washington | Ralph | B | 22-Aug-91 | 501 |
| 109 | Smith | Larry | W | 18-Jul-97 | 501 |

*Figure 15.2. Employee table with data for questions 4-10, by A. Watt.*

Use Figure 15.2 to answer questions 4 to 10.

4. Write the SQL code to change the job code to 501 for the person whose personnel number is 107. After you have completed the task, examine the results, and then reset the job code to its original value.
5. Assuming that the data shown in the Employee table have been entered, write the SQL code that lists all attributes for a job code of 502.
6. Write the SQL code to delete the row for the person named William Smithfield, who was hired on June 22, 2004, and whose job code classification is 500. (*Hint*: Use logical operators to include all the information given in this problem.)
7. Add the attributes EMP_PCT and PROJ_NUM to the Employee table. The EMP_PCT is the bonus percentage to be paid to each employee.
8. Using a single command, write the SQL code that will enter the project number (PROJ_NUM) = 18 for all employees whose job classification (JOB_CODE) is 500.
9. Using a single command, write the SQL code that will enter the project number (PROJ_NUM) = 25 for all employees whose job classification (JOB_CODE) is 502 or higher.
10. Write the SQL code that will change the PROJ_NUM to 14 for those employees who were hired before January 1, 1994, and whose job code is at least 501. (You may assume that the table will be restored to its original condition preceding this question.)

**Also see** *Appendix C: SQL Lab with Solution*

## References

Date, C.J. *Relational Database Selected Writings*. Reading: Mass: Addison-Wesley Publishing Company Inc., 1986, p. 269-311.

# Chapter 16 SQL Data Manipulation Language

The SQL data manipulation language (DML) is used to query and modify database data. In this chapter, we will describe how to use the SELECT, INSERT, UPDATE, and DELETE SQL DML command statements, defined below.

- *SELECT* – to query data in the database
- *INSERT* – to insert data into a table
- *UPDATE* – to update data in a table
- *DELETE* – to delete data from a table

In the SQL DML statement:

- Each clause in a statement should begin on a new line.
- The beginning of each clause should line up with the beginning of other clauses.
- If a clause has several parts, they should appear on separate lines and be indented under the start of the clause to show the relationship.
- Upper case letters are used to represent reserved words.
- Lower case letters are used to represent user-defined words.

## SELECT Statement

The SELECT statement, or command, allows the user to extract data from tables, based on specific criteria. It is processed according to the following sequence:

SELECT DISTINCT item(s)
FROM table(s)
WHERE predicate
GROUP BY field(s)
ORDER BY fields

We can use the SELECT statement to generate an employee phone list from the Employees table as follows:

```
SELECT FirstName, LastName, phone
FROM Employees
ORDER BY LastName
```

This action will display employee's last name, first name, and phone number from the Employees table, seen in Table 16.1.

| Last Name | First Name | Phone Number |
|---|---|---|
| Hagans | Jim | 604-232-3232 |
| Wong | Bruce | 604-244-2322 |

*Table 16.1. Employees table.*

In this next example, we will use a Publishers table (Table 16.2). (You will notice that Canada is mispelled in the *Publisher Country* field for Example Publishing and ABC Publishing. To correct mispelling, use the UPDATE statement to standardize the country field to Canada – see UPDATE statement later in this chapter.)

| Publisher Name | Publisher City | Publisher Province | Publisher Country |
|---|---|---|---|
| Acme Publishing | Vancouver | BC | Canada |
| Example Publishing | Edmonton | AB | Cnada |
| ABC Publishing | Toronto | ON | Canda |

*Table 16.2. Publishers table.*

If you add the publisher's name and city, you would use the SELECT statement followed by the fields name separated by a comma:

```
SELECT PubName, city
FROM Publishers
```

This action will display the publisher's name and city from the Publishers table.

If you just want the publisher's name under the display name city, you would use the SELECT statement with *no comma* separating pub_name and city:

```
SELECT PubName city
FROM Publishers
```

Performing this action will display only the pub_name from the Publishers table with a "city" heading. If you do not include the comma, SQL Server assumes you want a new column name for pub_name.

## SELECT statement with WHERE criteria

Sometimes you might want to focus on a portion of the Publishers table, such as only publishers that are in Vancouver. In this situation, you would use the SELECT statement with the WHERE criterion, i.e., WHERE city = 'Vancouver'.

These first two examples illustrate how to limit record selection with the WHERE criterion using BETWEEN. Each of these examples give the same results for store items with between 20 and 50 items in stock.

Example #1 uses the quantity, *qty* BETWEEN 20 *and* 50.

```
SELECT StorID, qty, TitleID
FROM Sales
WHERE qty BETWEEN 20 and 50  (includes the 20 and 50)
```

Example #2, on the other hand, uses *qty* >=20 *and qty* <=50 .

```
SELECT StorID, qty, TitleID
FROM Sales
WHERE qty >= 20 and qty  <= 50
```

Example #3 illustrates how to limit record selection with the WHERE criterion using NOT BETWEEN.

```
SELECT StorID, qty, TitleID
FROM Sales
WHERE qty NOT BETWEEN 20 and 50
```

The next two examples show two different ways to limit record selection with the WHERE criterion using IN, with each yielding the same results.

Example #4 shows how to select records using *province*= as part of the WHERE statement.

```
SELECT *
FROM Publishers
WHERE province = ‘BC’ OR province = ‘AB’ OR province = ‘ON’
```

Example #5 select records using *province* IN as part of the WHERE statement.

```
SELECT *
FROM Publishers
WHERE province IN (‘BC’, ‘AB’, ‘ON’)
```

The final two examples illustrate how NULL and NOT NULL can be used to select records. For these examples, a

Books table (not shown) would be used that contains fields called Title, Quantity, and Price (of book). Each publisher has a Books table that lists all of its books.

Example #6 uses NULL.

```
SELECT price, title
FROM Books
WHERE price IS NULL
```

Example #7 uses NOT NULL.

```
SELECT price, title
FROM Books
WHERE price IS NOT NULL
```

## Using wildcards in the LIKE clause

The LIKE keyword selects rows containing fields that match specified portions of character strings. LIKE is used with char, varchar, text, datetime and smalldatetime data. A *wildcard* allows the user to match fields that contain certain letters. For example, the wildcard province = 'N%' would give all provinces that start with the letter 'N'. Table 16.3 shows four ways to specify wildcards in the SELECT statement in regular express format.

| | |
|---|---|
| % | Any string of zero or more characters |
| _ | Any single character |
| [ ] | Any single character within the specified range (e.g., [a-f]) or set (e.g., [abcdef]) |
| [^] | Any single character not within the specified range (e.g., [^a – f]) or set (e.g., [^abcdef]) |

*Table 16.3. How to specify wildcards in the SELECT statement.*

In example #1, LIKE 'Mc%' searches for all last names that begin with the letters "Mc" (e.g., McBadden).

```
SELECT LastName
FROM Employees
WHERE LastName LIKE 'Mc%'
```

For example #2: LIKE '%inger' searches for all last names that end with the letters "inger" (e.g., Ringer, Stringer).

```
SELECT LastName
FROM Employees
WHERE LastName LIKE '%inger'
```

In, example #3: LIKE '%en%' searches for all last names that have the letters "en" (e.g., Bennett, Green, McBadden).

```
SELECT LastName
FROM Employees
WHERE LastName LIKE '%en%'
```

## SELECT statement with ORDER BY clause

You use the ORDER BY clause to sort the records in the resulting list. Use ASC to sort the results in ascending order and DESC to sort the results in descending order.

For example, with ASC:

```
SELECT *
FROM Employees
ORDER BY HireDate ASC
```

And with DESC:

```
SELECT *
FROM Books
ORDER BY type, price DESC
```

## SELECT statement with GROUP BY clause

The GROUP BY clause is used to create one output row per each group and produces summary values for the selected columns, as shown below.

```
SELECT type
FROM Books
GROUP BY type
```

Here is an example using the above statement.

```
SELECT type AS 'Type', MIN(price) AS 'Minimum Price'
FROM Books
WHERE royalty > 10
GROUP BY type
```

If the SELECT statement includes a WHERE criterion where *price is not null*,

```
SELECT type, price
FROM Books
WHERE price is not null
```

then a statement with the GROUP BY clause would look like this:

```
SELECT type AS 'Type', MIN(price) AS 'Minimum Price'
FROM Books
WHERE price is not null
GROUP BY type
```

## Using COUNT with GROUP BY

We can use COUNT to tally how many items are in a container. However, if we want to count different items into separate groups, such as marbles of varying colours, then we would use the COUNT function with the GROUP BY command.

The below SELECT statement illustrates how to count groups of data using the COUNT function with the GROUP BY clause.

```
SELECT COUNT(*)
FROM Books
GROUP BY type
```

## Using AVG and SUM with GROUP BY

We can use the AVG function to give us the average of any group, and SUM to give the total.

Example #1 uses the AVG FUNCTION with the GROUP BY type.

```
SELECT AVG(qty)
FROM Books
GROUP BY type
```

Example #2 uses the SUM function with the GROUP BY type.

```
SELECT SUM(qty)
FROM Books
GROUP BY type
```

Example #3 uses both the AVG and SUM functions with the GROUP BY type in the SELECT statement.

```
SELECT 'Total Sales' = SUM(qty), 'Average Sales' = AVG(qty), stor_id
FROM Sales
GROUP BY StorID ORDER BY  'Total Sales'
```

## Restricting rows with HAVING

The HAVING clause can be used to restrict rows. It is similar to the WHERE condition except HAVING can include the aggregate function; the WHERE cannot do this.

The HAVING clause behaves like the WHERE clause, but is applicable to groups. In this example, we use the HAVING clause to exclude the groups with the province 'BC'.

```
SELECT au_fname AS ‘Author”s First Name’, province as ‘Province’
FROM Authors
GROUP BY au_fname, province
HAVING province <> ‘BC’
```

## INSERT statement

The INSERT *statement* adds rows to a table. In addition,

- INSERT specifies the table or view that data will be inserted into.
- Column_list lists columns that will be affected by the INSERT.
- If a column is omitted, each value must be provided.
- If you are including columns, they can be listed in any order.
- VALUES specifies the data that you want to insert into the table. VALUES is required.
- Columns with the IDENTITY property should not be explicitly listed in the column_list or values_clause.

The syntax for the INSERT statement is:

```
INSERT [INTO] Table_name | view name [column_list]
DEFAULT VALUES | values_list | select statement
```

When inserting rows with the INSERT statement, these rules apply:

- Inserting an empty string (‘ ‘) into a varchar or text column inserts a single space.
- All char columns are right-padded to the defined length.
- All trailing spaces are removed from data inserted into varchar columns, except in strings that contain only spaces. These strings are truncated to a single space.
- If an INSERT statement violates a constraint, default or rule, or if it is the wrong data type, the statement fails and SQL Server displays an error message.

When you specify values for only some of the columns in the column_list, one of three things can happen to the columns that have no values:

1. A default value is entered if the column has a DEFAULT constraint, if a default is bound to the column, or if a default is bound to the underlying user-defined data type.
2. NULL is entered if the column allows NULLs and no default value exists for the column.
3. An error message is displayed and the row is rejected if the column is defined as NOT NULL and no default exists.

This example uses INSERT to add a record to the publisher’s Authors table.

```
INSERT INTO Authors
VALUES('555-093-467', 'Martin', 'April', '281 555-5673', '816 Market St.,' , 'Vancouver', 'BC', 'V7G3P4', 0)
```

This following example illustrates how to insert a partial row into the Publishers table with a column list. The country column had a default value of Canada so it does not require that you include it in your values.

```
INSERT INTO Publishers (PubID, PubName, city, province)
VALUES ('9900', 'Acme Publishing', 'Vancouver', 'BC')
```

To insert rows into a table with an IDENTITY column, follow the below example. Do not supply the value for the IDENTITY nor the name of the column in the column list.

```
INSERT INTO jobs
VALUES ('DBA', 100, 175)
```

## Inserting specific values into an IDENTITY column

By default, data cannot be inserted directly into an IDENTITY column; however, if a row is accidentally deleted, or there are gaps in the IDENTITY column values, you can insert a row and specify the IDENTITY column value.

```
IDENTITY_INSERT option
```

To allow an insert with a specific identity value, the IDENTITY_INSERT option can be used as follows.

```
SET IDENTITY_INSERT jobs ON
INSERT INTO jobs  (job_id, job_desc, min_lvl, max_lvl)
VALUES (19, 'DBA2', 100, 175)
SET IDENTITY_INSERT jobs OFF
```

## Inserting rows with a SELECT statement

We can sometimes create a small temporary table from a large table. For this, we can insert rows with a SELECT statement. When using this command, there is no validation for uniqueness. Consequently, there may be many rows with the same pub_id in the example below.

This example creates a smaller temporary Publishers table using the CREATE TABLE statement. Then the INSERT with a SELECT statement is used to add records to this temporary Publishers table from the publis table.

```
CREATE TABLE dbo.tmpPublishers (
PubID char (4) NOT NULL ,
PubName varchar (40) NULL ,
city varchar (20) NULL ,
province char (2) NULL ,
country varchar (30) NULL  DEFAULT ('Canada')
)
INSERT  tmpPublishers
SELECT * FROM Publishers
```

In this example, we're copying a subset of data.

```
INSERT tmpPublishers (pub_id, pub_name)
SELECT PubID, PubName
FROM Publishers
```

In this example, the publishers' data are copied to the tmpPublishers table and the country column is set to Canada.

```
INSERT tmpPublishers (PubID, PubName, city, province, country)
SELECT PubID, PubName, city, province, 'Canada'
FROM Publishers
```

## UPDATE statement

The UPDATE *statement* changes data in existing rows either by adding new data or modifying existing data.

This example uses the UPDATE statement to standardize the country field to be Canada for all records in the Publishers table.

```
UPDATE Publishers
SET country = 'Canada'
```

This example increases the royalty amount by 10% for those royalty amounts between 10 and 20.

```
UPDATE roysched
SET royalty = royalty + (royalty * .10)
WHERE royalty BETWEEN 10 and 20
```

### Including subqueries in an UPDATE statement

The employees from the Employees table who were hired by the publisher in 2010 are given a promotion to the highest job level for their job type. This is what the UPDATE statement would look like.

```
UPDATE Employees
SET job_lvl =
(SELECT max_lvl FROM jobs
WHERE employee.job_id = jobs.job_id)
WHERE DATEPART(year, employee.hire_date) = 2010
```

## DELETE statement

The DELETE *statement* removes rows from a record set. DELETE names the table or view that holds the rows that will be deleted and only one table or row may be listed at a time. WHERE is a standard WHERE clause that limits the deletion to select records.

The DELETE syntax looks like this.

```
DELETE [FROM] {table_name | view_name }
[WHERE clause]
```

The rules for the DELETE statement are:

1. If you omit a WHERE clause, all rows in the table are removed (except for indexes, the table, constraints).
2. DELETE cannot be used with a view that has a FROM clause naming more than one table. (Delete can affect only one base table at a time.)

What follows are three different DELETE statements that can be used.

1. Deleting all rows from a table.

```
DELETE
FROM Discounts
```

2. Deleting selected rows:

```
DELETE
FROM Sales
WHERE stor_id = '6380'
```

3. Deleting rows based on a value in a subquery:

```
DELETE FROM Sales
WHERE title_id IN
(SELECT title_id FROM Books WHERE type = 'mod_cook')
```

## Built-in Functions

There are many built-in functions in SQL Server such as:

1. *Aggregate*: returns summary values
2. *Conversion:* transforms one data type to another
3. *Date:* displays information about dates and times
4. *Mathematical:* performs operations on numeric data
5. *String*: performs operations on character strings, binary data or expressions
6. *System*: returns a special piece of information from the database
7. *Text and image*: performs operations on text and image data

Below you will find detailed descriptions and examples for the first four functions.

## Aggregate functions

Aggregate functions perform a calculation on a set of values and return a single, or summary, value. Table 16.4 lists these functions.

| FUNCTION | DESCRIPTION |
|---|---|
| AVG | Returns the average of all the values, or only the DISTINCT values, in the expression. |
| COUNT | Returns the number of non-null values in the expression. When DISTINCT is specified, COUNT finds the number of unique non-null values. |
| COUNT(*) | Returns the number of rows. COUNT(*) takes no parameters and cannot be used with DISTINCT. |
| MAX | Returns the maximum value in the expression. MAX can be used with numeric, character and datetime columns, but not with bit columns. With character columns, MAX finds the highest value in the collating sequence. MAX ignores any null values. |
| MIN | Returns the minimum value in the expression. MIN can be used with numeric, character and datetime columns, but not with bit columns. With character columns, MIN finds the value that is lowest in the sort sequence. MIN ignores any null values. |
| SUM | Returns the sum of all the values, or only the DISTINCT values, in the expression. SUM can be used with numeric columns only. |

*Table 16.4 A list of aggregate functions and descriptions.*

Below are examples of each of the aggregate functions listed in Table 16.4.

**Example #1: AVG**

```
SELECT AVG (price) AS 'Average Title Price'
FROM Books
```

**Example #2: COUNT**

```
SELECT COUNT(PubID) AS 'Number of Publishers'
FROM Publishers
```

**Example #3: COUNT**

```
SELECT COUNT(province) AS 'Number of Publishers'
FROM Publishers
```

**Example #3: COUNT (*)**

```
SELECT COUNT(*)
FROM Employees
WHERE job_lvl = 35
```

**Example #4: MAX**

```
SELECT MAX (HireDate)
FROM Employees
```

**Example #5: MIN**

```
SELECT MIN (price)
FROM Books
```

**Example #6: SUM**

```
SELECT SUM(discount) AS 'Total Discounts'
FROM Discounts
```

## Conversion function

The conversion function transforms one data type to another.

In the example below, a price that contains two 9s is converted into five characters. The syntax for this statement is SELECT 'The date is ' + CONVERT(varchar(12), getdate()).

```
SELECT CONVERT(int, 10.6496)
SELECT title_id, price
FROM Books
WHERE CONVERT(char(5), price) LIKE '%99%'
```

In this second example, the conversion function changes data to a data type with a different size.

```
SELECT title_id, CONVERT(char(4), ytd_sales) as 'Sales'
FROM Books
WHERE type LIKE '%cook'
```

## Date function

The date function produces a date by adding an interval to a specified date. The result is a datetime value equal to the date plus the number of date parts. If the date parameter is a smalldatetime value, the result is also a smalldatetime value.

The DATEADD function is used to add and increment date values. The syntax for this function is DATEADD(datepart, number, date).

```
SELECT DATEADD(day, 3, hire_date)
FROM Employees
```

In this example, the function DATEDIFF(datepart, date1, date2) is used.

This command returns the number of datepart "boundaries" crossed between two specified dates. The method of counting crossed boundaries makes the result given by DATEDIFF consistent across all data types such as minutes, seconds, and milliseconds.

```
SELECT DATEDIFF(day, HireDate, 'Nov 30 1995')
FROM Employees
```

For any particular date, we can examine any part of that date from the year to the millisecond.

The date parts (DATEPART) and abbreviations recognized by SQL Server, and the acceptable values are listed in Table 16.5.

| DATE PART | ABBREVIATION | VALUES |
|---|---|---|
| Year | yy | 1753-9999 |
| Quarter | qq | 1-4 |
| Month | mm | 1-12 |
| Day of year | dy | 1-366 |
| Day | dd | 1-31 |
| Week | wk | 1-53 |
| Weekday | dw | 1-7 (Sun.-Sat.) |
| Hour | hh | 0-23 |
| Minute | mi | 0-59 |
| Second | ss | 0-59 |
| Millisecond | ms | 0-999 |

*Table 16.5. Date part abbreviations and values.*

## Mathematical functions

Mathematical functions perform operations on numeric data. The following example lists the current price for each book sold by the publisher and what they would be if all prices increased by 10%.

```
SELECT Price, (price * 1.1) AS 'New Price', title
FROM Books
SELECT 'Square Root' = SQRT(81)
SELECT 'Rounded' = ROUND(4567.9876,2)
SELECT FLOOR (123.45)
```

# Joining Tables

Joining two or more tables is the process of comparing the data in specified columns and using the comparison results to form a new table from the rows that qualify. A join statement:

- Specifies a column from each table
- Compares the values in those columns row by row
- Combines rows with qualifying values into a new row

Although the comparison is usually for equality – values that match exactly – other types of joins can also be specified. All the different joins such as inner, left (outer), right (outer), and cross join will be described below.

## Inner join

An *inner join* connects two tables on a column with the same data type. Only the rows where the column values match are returned; unmatched rows are discarded.

**Example #1**

```
SELECT jobs.job_id, job_desc
FROM jobs
INNER JOIN Employees ON employee.job_id = jobs.job_id
WHERE jobs.job_id < 7
```

**Example #2**

```
SELECT authors.au_fname, authors.au_lname, books.royalty, title
FROM authorsINNER JOIN titleauthor ON authors.au_id=titleauthor.au_id
INNER JOIN books ON titleauthor.title_id=books.title_id
GROUP BY authors.au_lname, authors.au_fname, title, title.royalty
ORDER BY authors.au_lname
```

## Left outer join

A *left outer join* specifies that all left outer rows be returned. All rows from the left table that did not meet the condition specified are included in the results set, and output columns from the other table are set to NULL.

This first example uses the new syntax for a left outer join.

```
SELECT publishers.pub_name, books.title
FROM Publishers
LEFT OUTER JOIN Books On publishers.pub_id = books.pub_id
```

This is an example of a left outer join using the old syntax.

```
SELECT publishers.pub_name, books.title
FROM Publishers, Books
```

```
WHERE publishers.pub_id *= books.pub_id
```

## Right outer join

A *right outer join* includes, in its result set, all rows from the right table that did not meet the condition specified. Output columns that correspond to the other table are set to NULL.

Below is an example using the new syntax for a right outer join.

```
SELECT titleauthor.title_id, authors.au_lname, authors.au_fname
FROM titleauthor
RIGHT OUTER JOIN authors ON titleauthor.au_id = authors.au_id
ORDERY BY au_lname
```

This second example show the old syntax used for a right outer join.

```
SELECT titleauthor.title_id, authors.au_lname, authors.au_fname
FROM titleauthor, authors
WHERE titleauthor.au_id =* authors.au_id
ORDERY BY au_lname
```

## Full outer join

A *full outer join* specifies that if a row from either table does not match the selection criteria, the row is included in the result set, and its output columns that correspond to the other table are set to NULL.

Here is an example of a full outer join.

```
SELECT books.title, publishers.pub_name, publishers.province
FROM Publishers
FULL OUTER JOIN Books ON books.pub_id = publishers.pub_id
WHERE (publishers.province <> “BC” and publishers.province <> “ON”)
ORDER BY books.title_id
```

## Cross join

A *cross join* is a product combining two tables. This join returns the same rows as if no WHERE clause were specified. For example:

```
SELECT au_lname, pub_name,
FROM Authors CROSS JOIN Publishers
```

*Key Terms*

**aggregate function**: returns summary values**ASC**: ascending order

**conversion function**: transforms one data type to another

**cross join**: a product combining two tables

**date function**: displays information about dates and times

**DELETE statement**: removes rows from a record set

**DESC**: descending order

**full outer join**: specifies that if a row from either table does not match the selection criteria

**GROUP BY**: used to create one output row per each group and produces summary values for the selected columns

**inner join**: connects two tables on a column with the same data type

**INSERT statement**: adds rows to a table

**left outer join**: specifies that all left outer rows be returned

**mathematical function**: performs operations on numeric data

**right outer join**: includes all rows from the right table that did not meet the condition specified

**SELECT statemen**t: used to query data in the database

**string function**: performs operations on character strings, binary data or expressions

**system function**: returns a special piece of information from the database

**text and image functions**: performs operations on text and image data

**UPDATE statement:** changes data in existing rows either by adding new data or modifying existing data

**wildcard**: allows the user to match fields that contain certain letters.

*Exercises*

For questions 1 to 18 use the PUBS sample database created by Microsoft. To download the script to generate this database please go to the following site: http://www.microsoft.com/en-ca/download/details.aspx?id=23654.

1. Display a list of publication dates and titles (books) that were published in 2011.
2. Display a list of titles that have been categorized as either traditional or modern cooking. Use the Books table.
3. Display all authors whose first names are five letters long.
4. Display from the Books table: type, price, pub_id, title about the books put out by each publisher. Rename the column type with "Book Category." Sort by type (descending) and then price (ascending).
5. Display title_id, pubdate and pubdate plus three days, using the Books table.
6. Using the datediff and getdate function determine how much time has elapsed in months since the books in the Books table were published.
7. List the title IDs and quantity of all books that sold more than 30 copies.
8. Display a list of all last names of the authors who live in Ontario (ON) and the cities where they live.
9. Display all rows that contain a 60 in the payterms field. Use the Sales table.
10. Display all authors whose first names are five letters long , end in O or A, and start with M or P.
11. Display all titles that cost more than $30 and either begin with T or have a publisher ID of 0877.
12. Display from the Employees table the first name (fname), last name (lname), employe ID(emp_id) and job level (job_lvl) columns for those employees with a job level greater than 200; and rename the column headings to: "First Name," "Last Name," "IDENTIFICATION#" and "Job Level."
13. Display the royalty, royalty plus 50% as "royalty plus 50" and title_id. Use the Roysched table.
14. Using the STUFF function create a string "12xxxx567" from the string "1234567."
15. Display the first 40 characters of each title, along with the average monthly sales for that title to date (ytd_sales/12). Use the Title table.
16. Show how many books have assigned prices.
17. Display a list of cookbooks with the average cost for all of the books of each type. Use the GROUP BY.

*Advanced Questions (Union, Intersect, and Minus)*

1. The relational set operators UNION, INTERSECT and MINUS work properly only if the relations are union-compatible. What does union-compatible mean, and how would you check for this condition?
2. What is the difference between UNION and UNION ALL? Write the syntax for each.
3. Suppose that you have two tables, Employees and Employees_1. The Employees table contains the records for three employees: Alice Cordoza, John Cretchakov, and Anne McDonald. The Employees_1 table contains the records for employees: John Cretchakov and Mary Chen. Given that information, what

is the query output for the UNION query? List the query output.

4. Given the employee information in question 3, what is the query output for the UNION ALL query? List the query output.
5. Given the employee information in question 3, what is the query output for the INTERSECT query? List the query output.
6. Given the employee information in question 3, what is the query output for the EXCEPT query? List the query output.
7. What is a cross join? Give an example of its syntax.
8. Explain these three join types:
   1. left outer join
   2. right outer join
   3. full outer join
9. What is a subquery, and what are its basic characteristics?
10. What is a correlated subquery? Give an example.
11. Suppose that a Product table contains two attributes, PROD_CODE and VEND_CODE. The values for the PROD_CODE are: ABC, DEF, GHI and JKL. These are matched by the following values for the VEND_CODE: 125, 124, 124 and 123, respectively (e.g., PROD_CODE value ABC corresponds to VEND_CODE value 125). The Vendor table contains a single attribute, VEND_CODE, with values 123, 124, 125 and 126. (The VEND_CODE attribute in the Product table is a foreign key to the VEND_CODE in the Vendor table.)
12. Given the information in question 11, what would be the query output for the following? Show values.
    1. A UNION query based on these two tables
    2. A UNION ALL query based on these two tables
    3. An INTERSECT query based on these two tables
    4. A MINUS query based on these two tables

*Advanced Questions (Using Joins)*

1. Display a list of all titles and sales numbers in the Books and Sales tables, including titles that have no sales. Use a join.
2. Display a list of authors' last names and all associated titles that each author has published sorted by the author's last name. Use a join. Save it as a view named: Published Authors.
3. Using a subquery, display all the authors (show last and first name, postal code) who receive a royalty of 100% and live in Alberta. Save it as a view titled: AuthorsView. When creating the view, rename the author's last name and first name as 'Last Name' and 'First Name'.
4. Display the stores that did not sell the title *Is Anger the Enemy*?
5. Display a list of store names for sales after 2013 (Order Date is greater than 2013). Display store name and order date.

6. Display a list of titles for books sold in store name "News & Brews." Display store name, titles and order dates.
7. List total sales (qty) by title. Display total quantity and title columns.
8. List total sales (qty) by type. Display total quantity and type columns.
9. List total sales (qty*price) by type. Display total dollar value and type columns.
10. Calculate the total number of types of books by publisher. Show publisher name and total count of types of books for each publisher.
11. Show publisher names that do not have any type of book. Display publisher name only.

# Appendix A University Registration Data Model Example

Here is a statement of the data requirements for a product to support the registration of and provide help to students of a fictitious e-learning university.

An e-learning university needs to keep details of its students and staff, the courses that it offers and the performance of the students who study its courses. The university is administered in four geographical regions (England, Scotland, Wales and Northern Ireland).

Information about each student should be initially recorded at registration. This includes the student's identification number issued at the time, name, year of registration and the region in which the student is located. A student is not required to enroll in any courses at registration; enrollment in a course can happen at a later time.

Information recorded for each member of the tutorial and counseling staff must include the staff number, name and region in which he or she is located. Each staff member may act as a counselor to one or more students, and may act as a tutor to one or more students on one or more courses. It may be the case that, at any particular point in time, a member of staff may not be allocated any students to tutor or counsel.

Each student has one counselor, allocated at registration, who supports the student throughout his or her university career. A student is allocated a separate tutor for each course in which he or she is enrolled. A staff member may only counsel or tutor a student who is resident in the same region as that staff member.

Each course that is available for study must have a course code, a title and a value in terms of credit points. A course is either a 15-point course or a 30-point course. A course may have a quota for the number of students enrolled in it at any one presentation. A course need not have any students enrolled in it (such as a course that has just been written and offered for study).

Students are constrained in the number of courses they can be enrolled in at any one time. They may not take courses simultaneously if their combined points total exceeds 180 points.

For assessment purposes, a 15-point course may have up to three assignments per presentation and a 30-point course may have up to five assignments per presentation. The grade for an assignment on any course is recorded as a mark out of 100.

The university database below is one possible data model that describes the above set of requirements. The model has several parts, beginning with an ERD and followed by a written description of entity types, constraints, and assumptions.

## Design Process

See Figure A.1.

1. The first step is to determine the kernels. These are typically nouns: Staff, Course, Student and Assignment.
2. The next step is to document all attributes for each entity. This is where you need to ensure that all tables are properly normalized.
3. Create the initial ERD and review it with the users.

4. Make changes if needed after the ERD review.
5. Verify the ER model with users to finalize the design.

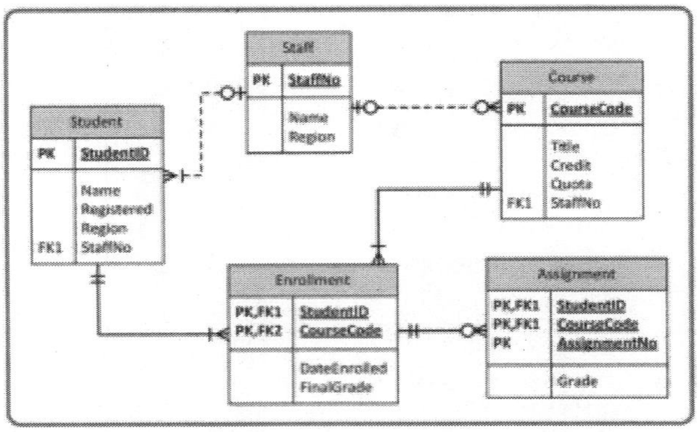


*Figure A.1. University ERD. A data model for a student and staff records system by A. Watt.*

## Entity

Student (StudentID, Name, Registered, Region, StaffNo)

Staff (StaffNo, Name, Region) – This table contains instructors and other staff members.

Course (CourseCode, Title, Credit, Quota, StaffNo)

Enrollment (StudentID, CourseCode, DateEnrolled, FinalGrade)

Assignment (StudentID, CourseCode, AssignmentNo, Grade)

## Constraints

- A staff member may only tutor or counsel students who are located in the same region as the staff member.
- Students may not enroll for more than 180 points worth of courses at any one time.
- The attribute Credit (of Course) has a value of 15 or 30 points.
- A 30-point course may have up to five assignments; a 15-point course may have up to three assignments.
- The attribute Grade (of Assignment) has a value that is a mark out of 100.

## Assumptions

- A student has at most one enrollment in a course as only current enrollments are recorded.
- An assignment may be submitted only once.

## Relationships (includes cardinality)

Using Figure A.2, note that a student (record) is associated with (enrolled) with a minimum of 1 to a maximum of many courses.

Each enrollment must have a valid student.

**Note:** Since the StudentID is part of the PK, it can't be null. Therefore, any StudentID entered, must exist in the Student table at least once to a maximum of 1 time. This should be obvious since the PK cannot have duplicates.

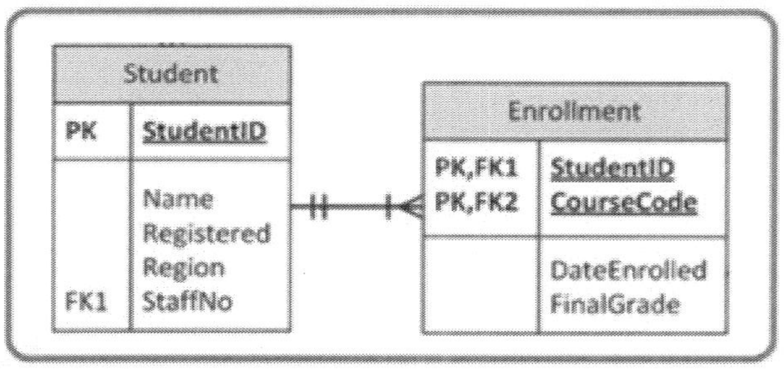


*Figure A.2 by A. Watt.*

Refer to Figure A.3. A staff record (a tutor) is associated with a minimum of 0 students to a maximum of many students.

A student record may or may not have a tutor.

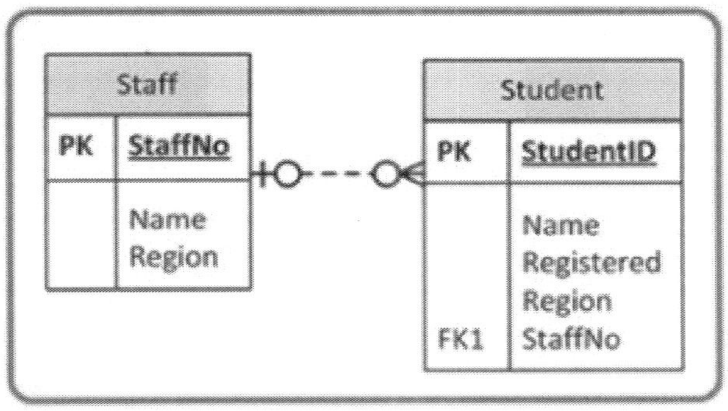


*Figure A.3 by A. Watt.*

**Note:** The StaffNo field in the Student table allows null values – represented by the 0 on the left side. However, if a StaffNo exists in the student table it must exist in the Staff table maximum once – represented by the 1.

Refer to Figure A.4. A staff record (instructor) is associated with a minimum of 0 courses to a maximum of many courses.

A course may or may not be associated with an instructor.

**Note:** The StaffNo in the Course table is the FK, and it can be null. This represents the 0 on the left side of the relationship. If the StaffNo has data, it has to be in the Staff table a maximum of once. That is represented by the 1 on the left side of the relationship.

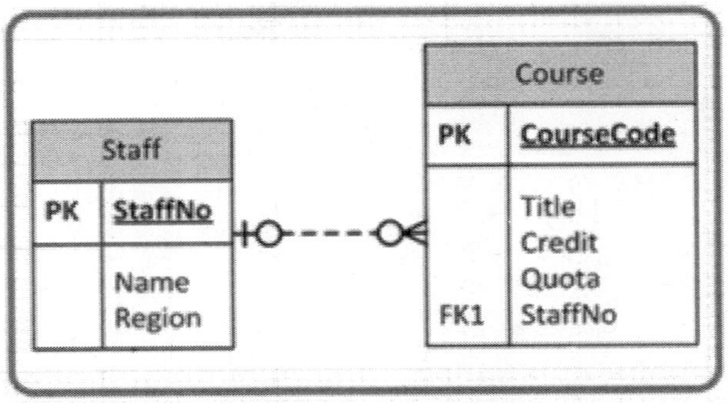


*Figure A.4 by A. Watt.*

Refer to Figure A.5. A course must be offered (in enrollment) at least once to a maximum of many times.

The Enrollment table must contain at least 1 valid course to a maximum of many.

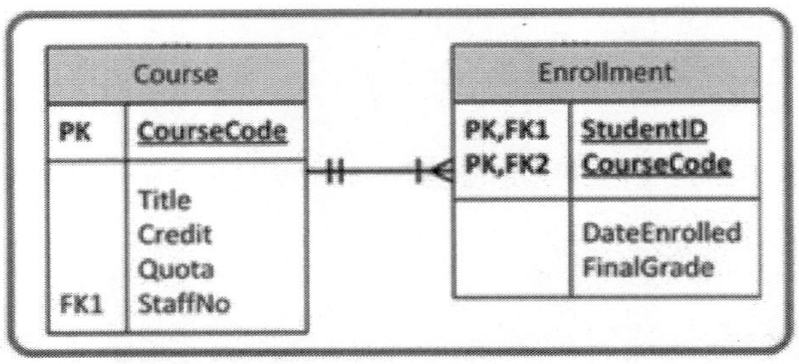


*Figure A.5 by A. Watt.*

Refer to Figure A.6. An enrollment can have a minimum of 0 assignments or a maximum of many.

An assignment must be associated with at least 1 with a maximum of 1 enrollment.

**Note:** Every record in the Assignment table must contain a valid enrollment record. One enrollment record can be associated with multiple assignments.

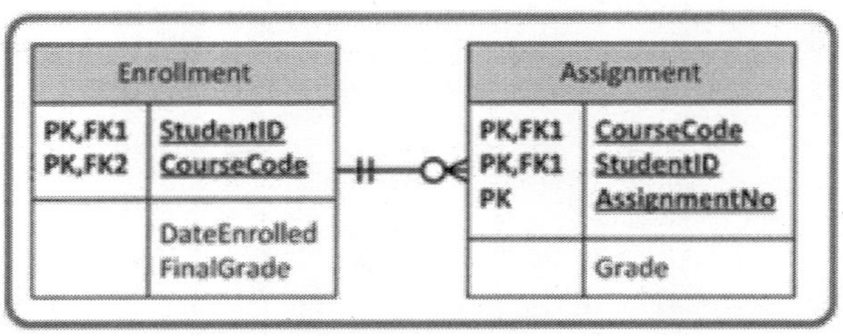


*Figure A.6 by A. Watt.*

## Attribution

This is an adaptation, not a derivation as the author wrote half of it. Source: http://openlearn.open.ac.uk/mod/oucontent/view.php?id=397581&section=8.2

# Appendix B Sample ERD Exercises

## Exercise 1

### Manufacturer

A manufacturing company produces products. The following product information is stored: product name, product ID and quantity on hand. These products are made up of many components. Each component can be supplied by one or more suppliers. The following component information is kept: component ID, name, description, suppliers who supply them, and products in which they are used. Use Figure B.1 for this exercise.

Create an ERD to show how you would track this information.

Show entity names, primary keys, attributes for each entity, relationships between the entities and cardinality.

### Assumptions

- A supplier can exist without providing components.
- A component does not have to be associated with a supplier.
- A component does not have to be associated with a product. Not all components are used in products.
- A product cannot exist without components.

### ERD Answer

Component(CompID, CompName, Description) PK=CompID

Product(ProdID, ProdName, QtyOnHand) PK=ProdID

Supplier(SuppID, SuppName) PK = SuppID

CompSupp(CompID, SuppID) PK = CompID, SuppID

Build(CompID, ProdID, QtyOfComp) PK= CompID, ProdID

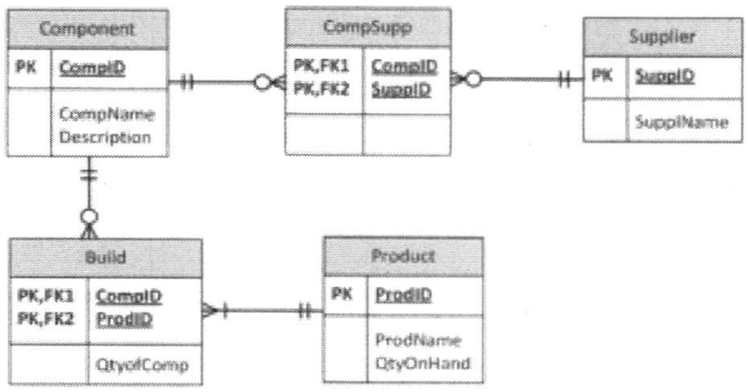


*Figure B.1 by A. Watt.*

## Exercise 2

### Car Dealership

Create an ERD for a car dealership. The dealership sells both new and used cars, and it operates a service facility (see Figure B.2). Base your design on the following business rules:

- A salesperson may sell many cars, but each car is sold by only one salesperson.
- A customer may buy many cars, but each car is bought by only one customer.
- A salesperson writes a single invoice for each car he or she sells.
- A customer gets an invoice for each car he or she buys.
- A customer may come in just to have his or her car serviced; that is, a customer need not buy a car to be classified as a customer.
- When a customer takes one or more cars in for repair or service, one service ticket is written for each car.
- The car dealership maintains a service history for each of the cars serviced. The service records are referenced by the car's serial number.
- A car brought in for service can be worked on by many mechanics, and each mechanic may work on many cars.
- A car that is serviced may or may not need parts (e.g., adjusting a carburetor or cleaning a fuel injector nozzle does not require providing new parts).

# ERD Answer

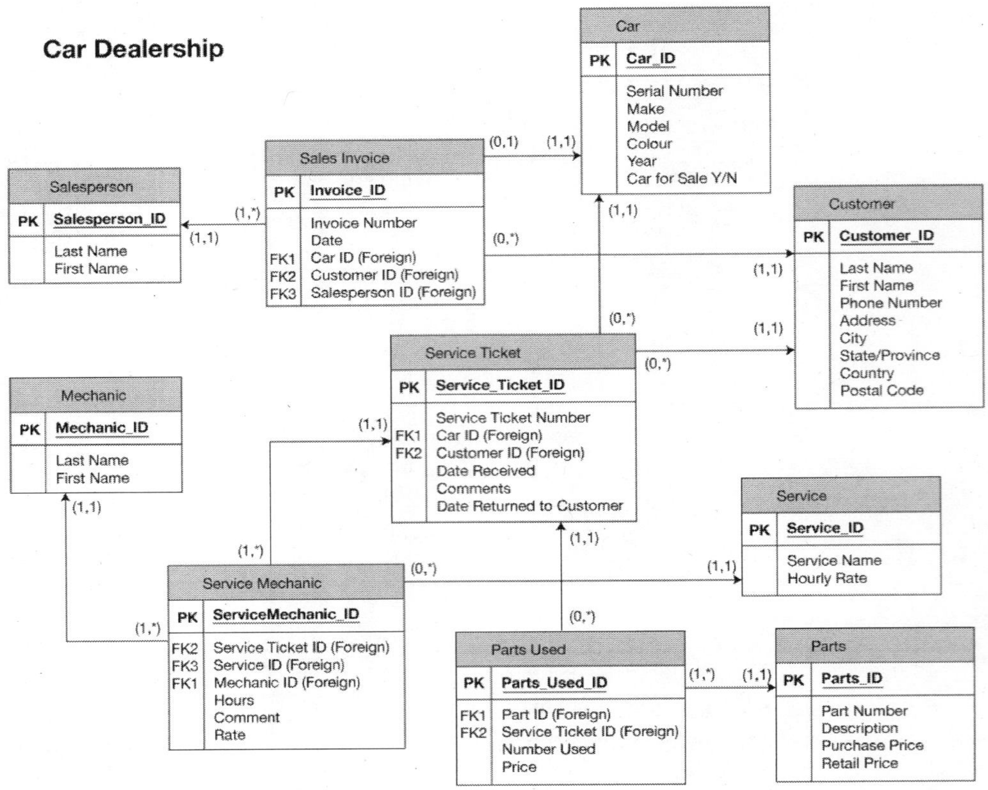

Car Dealership
Car
PK Car_ID
Serial Number
Make
Model
Colour
Year
Car for Sale Y/N
Sales Invoice
PK Invoice_ID
Invoice Number
Date
FK1 Car ID (Foreign)
FK2 Customer ID (Foreign)
FK3 Salesperson ID (Foreign)
Salesperson
PK Salesperson_ID
Last Name
First Name
Customer
PK Customer_ID
Last Name
First Name
Phone Number
Address
City
State/Province
Country
Postal Code
Service Ticket
PK Service_Ticket_ID
Service Ticket Number
FK1 Car ID (Foreign)
FK2 Customer ID (Foreign)
Date Received
Comments
Date Returned to Customer
Mechanic
PK Mechanic_ID
Last Name
First Name
Service
PK Service_ID
Service Name
Hourly Rate
Service Mechanic
PK ServiceMechanic_ID
FK2 Service Ticket ID (Foreign)
FK3 Service ID (Foreign)
FK1 Mechanic ID (Foreign)
Hours
Comment
Rate
Parts Used
PK Parts_Used_ID
FK1 Part ID (Foreign)
FK2 Service Ticket ID (Foreign)
Number Used
Price
Parts
PK Parts_ID
Part Number
Description
Purchase Price
Retail Price
(0,1) (1,1)
(1,*) (1,1)
(0,*) (1,1)
(1,1) (0,*)
(0,*) (1,1)
(1,1) (1,*)
(1,1) (1,*)
(0,*) (1,1)
(1,1) (0,*)
(1,*) (1,1)

# Appendix C SQL Lab with Solution

Download the following script: OrdersAndData.sql.

## Part 1 – DDL

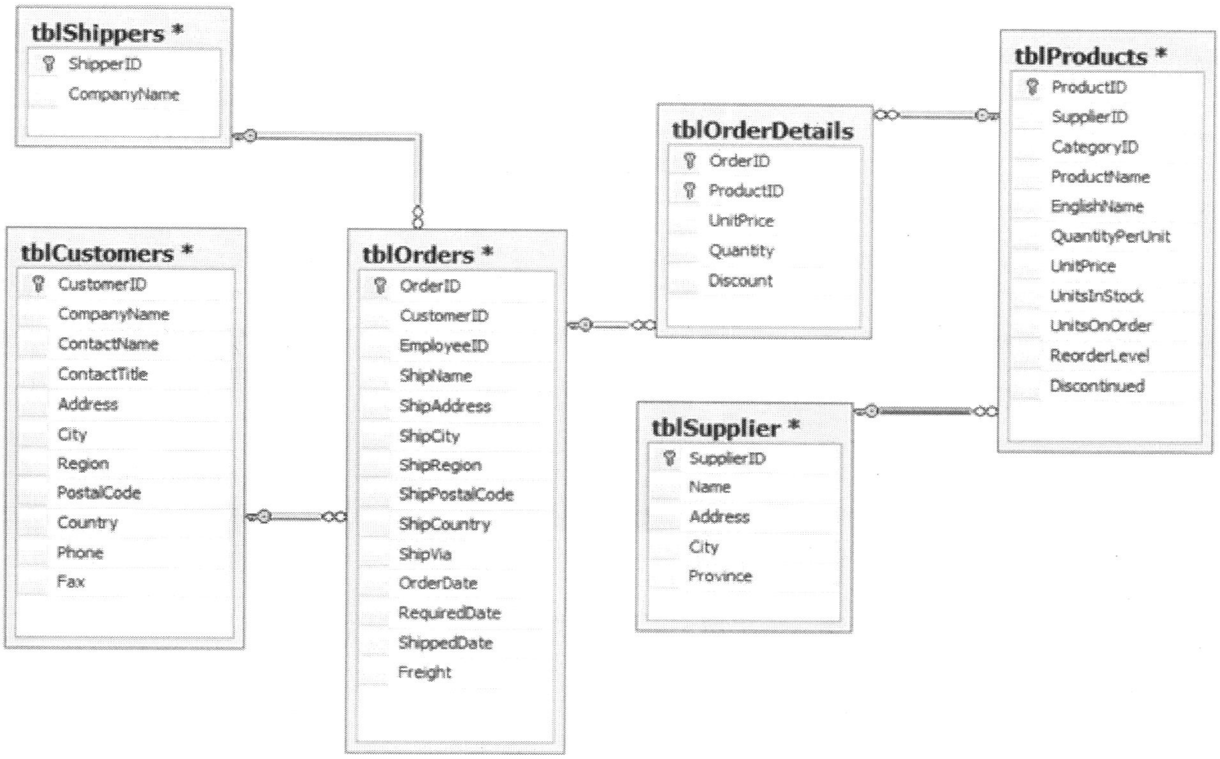


*Figure C.1. ERD for Orders and Data.*

1. Use the script OrdersAndData.sql that creates the tables and adds the data for the Orders and Data ERD in Figure C.1.
2. Create a database called Orders. Modify the script to integrate the PK and referential integrity. Show the CREATE TABLE statements with the modifications including the constraints given in step 3.
3. Add the following constraints:

- tblCustomers table: Country – default to Canada
- tblOrderDetails: Quantity – > 0
- tblShippers: CompanyName must be unique.
- tblOrders: ShippedDate must be greater than order date.

```
CREATE DATABASE Orders
Go
Use Orders
Go
```

```
Use Orders
Go
CREATE TABLE [dbo].[tblCustomers]
[CustomerID]       nvarchar(5) NOT NULL,
[CompanyName]      nvarchar(40) NOT NULL,
[ContactName]      nvarchar(30) NULL,
[ContactTitle]     nvarchar(30) NULL,
[Address]          nvarchar(60) NULL,
[City]             nvarchar(15) NULL,
[Region]           nvarchar(15) NULL,
[PostalCode]       nvarchar(10) NULL,
[Country]          nvarchar(15) NULL
Constraint    df_country DEFAULT 'Canada',
[Phone]            nvarchar(24) NULL,
[Fax]              nvarchar(24) NULL,
Primary Key (CustomerID)
);
```

```
CREATE TABLE [dbo].[tblSupplier] (
[SupplierID]     int NOT NULL,
[Name]           nvarchar(50) NULL,
[Address]        nvarchar(50) NULL,
[City]           nvarchar(50) NULL,
[Province]       nvarchar(50) NULL,
Primary Key (SupplierID)
);
```

```
CREATE TABLE [dbo].[tblShippers] (
[ShipperID]      int NOT NULL,
[CompanyName]    nvarchar(40) NOT NULL,
Primary Key (ShipperID),<
```

```
CONSTRAINT uc_CompanyName UNIQUE (CompanyName)
);
```

```
CREATE TABLE [dbo].[tblProducts] (
[ProductID]         int NOT NULL,
[SupplierID]        int NULL,
[CategoryID]        int NULL,
[ProductName]       nvarchar(40) NOT NULL,
[EnglishName]       nvarchar(40) NULL,
[QuantityPerUnit]   nvarchar(20) NULL,
[UnitPrice]         money NULL,
[UnitsInStock]      smallint NULL,
[UnitsOnOrder]      smallint NULL,
[ReorderLevel]      smallint NULL,
[Discontinued]      bit NOT NULL,
Primary Key (ProductID),
Foreign Key (SupplierID) References tblSupplier
);
```

```
CREATE TABLE [dbo].[tblOrders] (
[OrderID]           int NOT NULL,
[CustomerID]        nvarchar(5) NOT NULL,
[EmployeeID]        int NULL,
[ShipName]          nvarchar(40) NULL,
[ShipAddress]       nvarchar(60) NULL,
[ShipCity]          nvarchar(15) NULL,
[ShipRegion]        nvarchar(15) NULL,
[ShipPostalCode]    nvarchar(10) NULL,
[ShipCountry]       nvarchar(15) NULL,
[ShipVia]           int NULL,
[OrderDate]         smalldatetime NULL,
[RequiredDate]      smalldatetime NULL,
[ShippedDate]       smalldatetime NULL,
[Freight]           money NULL
Primary Key (OrderID),
Foreign Key (CustomerID) References tblCustomers,
Foreign Key (ShipVia) References tblShippers,
Constraint valid_ShipDate CHECK (ShippedDate > OrderDate)
);
```

```
CREATE TABLE [dbo].[tblOrderDetails] (
[OrderID]      int NOT NULL,
[ProductID]    int NOT NULL,
[UnitPrice]    money NOT NULL,
[Quantity]     smallint NOT NULL,
[Discount]     real NOT NULL,
Primary Key (OrderID, ProductID),
Foreign Key (OrderID) References tblOrders,
Foreign Key (ProductID) References tblProducts,
Constraint Valid_Qty Check (Quantity > 0)
);
Go
```

## Part 2 – Create the Following SQL Statements

1. Show a list of customers and the orders they generated during 2014. Display customer ID, order ID, order date and date ordered.

```
Use Orders
Go
SELECT CompanyName, OrderID, RequiredDate as 'order date', OrderDate as 'date ordered'
FROM tblcustomers  JOIN tblOrders on tblOrders.CustomerID = tblCustomers.CustomerID
WHERE Year(OrderDate) = 2014
```

2. Using the ALTER TABLE statement, add a new field (Active) in the tblcustomer. Default it to True.

```
ALTER TABLE tblCustomers
ADD Active bit DEFAULT ('True')
```

3. Show all orders purchased before September 1, 2012. Display company name, date ordered and total amount of order (include freight).

```
SELECT tblOrders.OrderID, OrderDate as 'Date Ordered', sum(unitprice*quantity*(1-discount))+ freight as
'Total Cost'
```

```
FROM tblOrderDetails join tblOrders on tblOrders.orderID = tblOrderDetails.OrderID
WHERE OrderDate < 'September 1, 2012'
GROUP BY tblOrders.OrderID, freight, OrderDate
```

4. Show all orders that have been shipped via Federal Shipping. Display OrderID, ShipName, ShipAddress and CustomerID.

```
SELECT OrderID, ShipName, ShipAddress, CustomerID
FROM tblOrders join tblShippers on tblOrders.ShipVia = tblShippers.ShipperID
WHERE CompanyName= 'Federal Shipping'
```

5. Show all customers who have not made purchases in 2011.

```
SELECT CompanyName
FROM tblCustomers
WHERE CustomerID not in
( SELECT CustomerID
FROM  tblOrders
WHERE Year(OrderDate) = 2011
)
```

6. Show all products that have never been ordered.

```
SELECT ProductID from tblProducts
Except
SELECT ProductID from tblOrderDetails
```

OR

```
SELECT Products.ProductID,Products.ProductName
FROM Products LEFT JOIN [Order Details]
ON Products.ProductID = [Order Details].ProductID
WHERE [Order Details].OrderID IS NULL
```

7. Show OrderIDs for customers who reside in London. Use a subquery. Display CustomerID, CustomerName and OrderID.

```
SELECT Customers.CompanyName,Customers.CustomerID,OrderID
FROM Orders
LEFT JOIN Customers ON Orders.CustomerID = Customers.CustomerID
WHERE Customers.CompanyName IN
(SELECT CompanyName
FROM Customers
WHERE City = 'London')
```

8. Show products supplied by Supplier A and Supplier B. Display product name and supplier name.

```
SELECT ProductName, Name
FROM tblProducts JOIN tblSupplier on tblProducts.SupplierID = tblSupplier.SupplierID
WHERE Name Like 'Supplier A' or Name Like 'Supplier B'
```

9. Show all products that come in boxes. Display product name and QuantityPerUnit.

```
SELECT EnglishName, ProductName,  QuantityPerUnit
FROM tblProducts
WHERE QuantityPerUnit like '%box%'
ORDER BY EnglishName
```

## Part 3 – Insert, Update, Delete, Indexes

1. Create an Employee table. The primary key should be EmployeeID (autonumber). Add the following fields: LastName, FirstName, Address, City, Province, Postalcode, Phone, Salary. Show the CREATE TABLE statement and the INSERT statements for the five employees. Join the employee table to the tblOrders. Show the script for creating the table, setting constraints and adding employees.

```
Use Orders
CREATE TABLE [dbo].[tblEmployee](
EmployeeID Int IDENTITY NOT NULL ,
FirstName varchar (20) NOT NULL,
```

```
LastName varchar (20) NOT NULL,
Address varchar (50),
City varchar(20), Province varchar (50),
PostalCode char(6),
Phone char (10),
Salary Money NOT NULL,
Primary Key (EmployeeID)
```

```
Go
INSERT into tblEmployees
Values ('Jim', 'Smith', '123 Fake', 'Terrace', 'BC', 'V8G5J6', '2506155989', '20.12'),
('Jimmy', 'Smithy', '124 Fake', 'Terrace', 'BC', 'V8G5J7', '2506155984', '21.12'),
('John', 'Smore', '13 Fake', 'Terrace', 'BC', 'V4G5J6', '2506115989', '19.12'),
('Jay', 'Sith', '12 Fake', 'Terrace', 'BC', 'V8G4J6', '2506155939', '25.12'),
('Jig', 'Mith', '23 Fake', 'Terrace', 'BC', 'V8G5J5', '2506455989', '18.12');
Go
```

2. Add a field to tblOrders called TotalSales. Show DDL – ALTER TABLE statement.

```
ALTER TABLE tblOrders
ADD Foreign Key (EmployeeID) references tblEmployees (EmployeeID)
```

3. Using the UPDATE statement, add the total sale for each order based on the order details table.

```
UPDATE tblOrders
Set TotalSales = (select sum(unitprice*quantity*(1-discount))
FROM tblOrderDetails
WHERE tblOrderDetails.OrderID= tblOrders.OrderID
GROUP BY OrderID
```

# Index

## G



## H



## I



## L



## M



## N



## P



## R



## S